MEDICAL ADMINISTRATION: MANAGEMENT TECHNIQUES

MEDICAL ADMINISTRATION: MANAGEMENT TECHNIQUES

by

A. Everette James, Jr., ScM., J.D., M.D.

Warren H. Green, Inc.
St. Louis, Missouri

Published by

WARREN H. GREEN, INC.
8356 Olive Boulevard
St. Louis, Missouri 63132, U.S.A.

ISBN No. 0-87527-511-7

Printed in the United States of America

DEDICATION

I am appreciative of the use of materials from my publications in *Administrative Radiology, Diagnostic Imaging, Health Matrix, Humane Medicine*, and *Investigative Radiology*. I am especially indebted to mentors Bill Anlyan, Larry Robbins, Russell Morgan, Henry Wagner, Martin Donner, Ike Robinson, John Chapman, Vernon Wilson, Alexander Heard, and Chris Fordham, and colleagues Charles Putman, Gerald Freedman, Bob White, Dick Heller, Henry Pendergrass, Leon Partain, David Rollo, Jim Blumstein, Terry Calvani, Hoyt Stephens, Raleigh Hamilton, the late M.D. Ingram, Jim Patton, Ron Price, Tom Greeson, and Otha Linton. My attorney children Everette James III and Jeannette James Whitson were helpful. My experiences at the University of North Carolina, Duke School of Medicine, 93rd Evac Hospital (SVN), the Massachusetts General Hospital, Johns Hopkins Institutions, University College (London), Harvard Business School, and Vanderbilt were a part of the learning process.

FORWARD

This text provides insights into the complexities of administration and management in medicine. The messages are conveyed in a series of vignettes written in a manner to provide the reader with an enjoyable learning experience. While the data is quite serious, there has been an attempt to "lighten" the experience. As far as I am aware, there is no competing text. Because it is written from a personal perspective, it is unique in this regard.

I hope this text will help, first, the administrators in any area of the health care field, and second, anyone wishing to become better informed about management strategy and administrative techniques.

Dr. A. Everette James ScM, M.D.

TABLE OF CONTENTS

MEDICAL ADMINISTRATION: MANAGEMENT TECHNIQUES

Chapter 1

ADMINISTRATIVE RESPONSE TO HEALTH CARE'S ENLARGED MANDATE

The complex disciplines of medicine occupy a unique position in the last decade of the 20th century. Our profession is challenged with ever-increasing regulation, asked to "do more with less," to respond to individual and collective consumerism, and to be accountable to a public that has become increasingly cynical, due to both information and misinformation regarding inconsistencies and inequities in our society. We must administrate our resources to the difference between limited and unavailable and come to recognize that our resources are not only finite, but those that we have will be regulated either externally or internally or both.

Administrators must appreciate the difference between responsive choices and expressions of taste from the public that we serve, and, in the case of service disciplines, this will involve the critical analysis of one's clinical colleagues. Their needs may well reflect their own tastes and, at times, outmoded beliefs expressed as demands based upon perceived mandates from their constituency, the patients.

Administrators must also recognize that they function in an uncertain environment and that their staff and faculty need to base their personal expectations on the reality in which they labor. If the economy of their region or area is weathering the vicissitudes of a significant recession, large increases in professional staff compensation may well be quite unrealistic. In a less global economic context (for example, that of a parent university), one should expect to meet the same financial challenges as the institution and not expect to be singled out for rewards of any type that are inconsistent with the environment in which they practice.

Physicians, as a subset of society, often feel that, due to their extraordinary training and sacrifice to acquire competence in their chosen endeavor, they should be accorded commensurate privileges and rewards. Today's social milieu may allow a part of this "separateness" but at the expense of a great deal of accountability and increasingly rigid standards of performance. Hence we experience the revelations of Medicare fraud and abuse, RBRVS, DRGs, and inquiries in expenditures of overhead from grants, fraud in research, and conflicts of interest. Today, physicians and departments can expect to be evaluated on performance, fees, record keeping, etc. by groups with no medical training or often quite limited experience in the health care field. The activities that we are required to engage in to earn the imprimatur of a particular agency, sanction of an evaluation group, or privileges to perform a special endeavor may have little or no apparent relevance to the actual practice of medicine and not closely reflect our previous training or experience. These requests and regulations often represent a policy response to an industry that has, in the view of many, become unbearably expensive, a privileged group of society that has too long been either unregulated or been allowed self regulation, and such an important part of our social fabric that the consumer must have a significant determinative role. Many of these challenges to medicine have such a global base and are derived from such fundamental societal changes that they cannot be left unanswered or ignored but must be understood for what they represent, responded to, and accommodated.

Our society has an interesting ambivalence to medical technology, for example. The intellectual fascination with the magnetic resonance imaging devices or the positron emission tomography scanner is a current example. However, with further knowledge acquired by the public regarding these biomedical engineering marvels has come some realization of the expense associated with these facilities as well as the individual studies and the need to establish their relative efficacy from a number of viewpoints before imposing the financial responsibility for their operation on the public.

Medicine (even the high tech variety) is increasingly being evaluated by policy makers as a commodity with a marketplace which is subject, in part, to free enterprise effects. The present administration now appears to favor the free enterprise/competitive model. Administrators will, in the future, accept the challenge of leading their staff and faculty in considering their profession as a calling but conducting many of their affairs as a business. External affirmation from a nurturing public will become less of a determinant of a physician's satisfaction than their own and their colleagues' assessment of their contribution. The luxury and prestige of ownership of a particular technology may not be realistic in the specific context in which a physician practices. The conduct of their professional activity may produce financial "winners and losers" and require an understanding of professional balance and the balance sheet. Whether or not a particular medical unit can provide a complete or limited service may well depend upon the monies available or the projected income to be derived from some potential service to be added. The new decisional basis may create anxiety, discomfort, and some resentment among the staff and faculty, requiring the administrative leadership to initiate positive steps to promote understanding and complicity, if not agreement.

While the mandate to reduce costs of medical care appears to require a reduction in technology use and future development, there is also the universal quest to maintain quality and provide access. Obviously, these are issues that are often interdependent and may not be achievable employing present or even conventional management and administrative techniques. Once again, the administrator must understand the global considerations that led to the challenging policy, value this in the context of the public interest, and then allocate and employ resources in a manner to best achieve or approximate the objective.

Taking MR imaging as an operative example, the cost of acquisition ($800,000-$2,500,000, depending on the magnet characteristics and site preparation) will increase society's interest that these facilities be efficiently utilized and that reasonable access be assured. To deprive a patient of such a unique and powerful device will not go unnoticed by any of the participants in the health care system (other providers, facility administrators, lenders, patients as consumers, regulators, and policy makers). The energy from the demand side may significantly alter the behavior from the supply side. In this mix, the guardian of technology must be responsive but maintain quality. Often, if the technology is not well established, the standards to assess efficacy or quality may not exist. Development of reasonable standards should be initiated by the practitioners and their administration, and management of the resources should reflect commitment to those guidelines. As standards and credentialling practices are promulgated by external agencies, the manager must be mindful of the quality goals and institute some method of ongoing evaluation to assure that quality will not be sacrificed for expediency. In a service-based discipline, the manager's communicative skills will be challenged by clinicians who are not as aware of or as interested in quality considerations. The maintenance of quality will be an ever-increasing dimension in an environment largely driven by performance demands.

Medicine's enlarged mandate requires that physicians not just diagnose and treat disease processes. Today, health care is a complex industry that provides additional challenges and often requires complicated responses. Besides the patient's welfare, the welfare of the facility or institution in which one's professional activities are conducted becomes very important. These latter responsibilities may involve financial/commercial considerations - a traditional anathema to medical leadership. The reduction of important quality decisions to purely economic criteria represents a difficult philosophical transition for most physicians. Accommodating the decisions rendered in both clinical and economic terms is difficult, and reasonably so when one recognizes that these are new interfaces. The enlarged mandate has not removed or moved medical administrators from the purely clinical area into the economic but has expanded the fundamental managerial considerations to include both. The immediacy of financial concerns and their quantifiable nature may sometimes have them appear as solely determinant. This should not be allowed by the medical administrator because, over time, quality must be maintained, and one should strive to meet the traditional criteria of standard of care. Administrative techniques may be significantly modified to respond to an enlarged mandate, but the historical values that have resulted in a history of adequate patient care still have present validity.

The purpose of this text is to apply certain managerial and administrative techniques to the complex and sometimes unique environment of health care. Hopefully, this will allow administrators and managers to serve their constituency with an emphasis upon care in its broadest context.

Chapter 2

THE TRANSITION FROM DOER TO FACILITATOR

The most difficult posture for many young or new administrators to assume is that of facilitator. In fact, many never do. After all, they probably achieved the lofty administrative status due to their own productivity and achievements. Certainly, this is yet another manifestation of The Peter Principle, in which the skills and talents that brought you to the party are not those that will necessarily make you successful in your present role. Thus, those attributes that allowed you to attain your position may not assist you in prospering in or even maintaining it.

In general, the route to the most responsible administrative positions in medicine is through scholarly achievement. Clinical skills are almost a judgement presumption by any search committee, and evaluation of interpersonal skills are often not a part of the decision process. Acclaim for original research and wide acceptance of publications are the paramount criteria in determining the suitability of a candidate for an administrative role in medicine. If asked, a search committee will give support to the consideration of candidates' "people skills" but will also realize that these are very difficult to judge — much less quantify. In turn, young staff realize early in their academic careers that the major advancement criteria are research and publications. They will engage actively in these activities, and it will soon become so much a part of their work ethic that it may also become their identity. Judging personal success and self worth may well be done in performance terms; hence, how one "is" may be how one "does." The private sector is a little more people oriented but not much.

After considerable experience as a successful producer, one is accorded the role of leader and administrator of others. The producer now has a choice, but many do not realize that options *are* available. Often a young administrator will continue to be a "doer" only, thinking that they are leading by example. In this role, they may continue to be personally productive on an academic level but will very likely fail to provide nurture and sustenance to the young members on their staff. Over time, the turnover among young, ambitious staff will be great, and the stature of the administrator will be arrested at the level they had achieved as a "doer/scholar." The young medical administrator has not departed from some well-conceived plan for ultimate success. Rather, they have followed a path that their previous achievements and their earlier environment indicated as the proper one.

Most people would reason that if one arrived at a certain administrative position by their own productivity, then they should continue these activities to maintain their fame. Besides, they have become proficient in this role and may only feel comfortable by continuing this posture, because it seems like the natural and the appropriate thing to do. However, this is a limiting administrative style and one that is destined to lower one's horizons.

Accepting the role of facilitator may be initially an uncomfortable task and one that a young administrator may soon abandon. It requires discipline to forego the instant gratification from accomplishing a task directly by your own efforts. You will predictably lament the lack of short-term rewards in your life and will, at first, find it difficult to summon the necessary patience of a facilitator. You must change from a task-oriented professional lifestyle to one in which the goal will be much less clearly defined. As a doer, your accomplishments were often quite well understood and recognized by others. You were a bit like an ultrasound transducer in that you could tell where you "were" by bouncing the signal off of others. As a facilitator, the returning signals, if there are any, are very unclear, and it is difficult even for you to tell where you "are." In fact, you had best decide where you are before you adopt the mantle of a facilitator.

Despite the fact that your administrative leadership may be well accepted, your skills as a facilitator may go largely unnoticed by those you lead. Pointing out your facilitation to those who benefit from your efforts will likely be viewed as self-serving and will almost certainly not produce a genuine response of gratitude. So if your staff criticizes the lack of resources in your facility, your response as facilitator is neither to defend where you are nor to be offended that they do not recognize how far you have come in this imperfect world. Your role as facilitator is to focus upon the validity of the alleged shortcomings and attempt to garner resources to correct those that are, indeed, real.

As the facilitator, you must take the long view in evaluating the performance of those you lead. While they may not respond to your administrative leadership as you would have wished, you simply cannot impose your will, aspirations, or style of performance upon others. To do so will obviate your facilitator role and may very well compromise your future position as administrative leader. So where do you, as the facilitator, derive your satisfaction and your rewards? These must lie in the achievements of others for whom you feel responsible. Eventually, the world may discover the merit and wisdom of your activities; but long before that you should have developed your own personal evaluation of your efforts from the accomplishments of the colleagues you administrate.

Chapter 3

SUPPORTING EXCELLENCE

Much has been made in the American system of free enterprise about the search for excellence. Almost equal attention has been devoted to administrative techniques leading to the creation of excellence. In medical administration, we have a somewhat different challenge: that of supporting excellence. The outcome does, indeed, create excellence, but in a quite different manner from a normal business enterprise. That is the concept I would like to explore in this communication.

The selection process from undergraduate admission to medical school entry through the rigors of residency, fellowship and, finally, board certification creates a group of individuals who have already achieved at least a form of excellence. More important to the administrator is that these individuals have the prerequisite skills, expertise and discipline to enlarge upon this excellence, provided they are placed in an environment that supports the growth. In Peters and Waterman's **In Search of Excellence**, the authors chronicle the characteristics of business and industrial enterprises that have been successful in this regard. For the administrator in medicine, it might prove useful to consider some of these in our more specific context of a response to patients' and other physicians' needs with the ultimate responsibility of financial solvency.

The psychologist, Ernest Becker, believes that we transcend death by finding meaning in our lives. We do not fear death so much as extinction without meaning or, conversely, insignificant meaning. Our sense of self worth is largely constituted in a symbolic fashion. A medical institution can provide the same symbols as an exclusive club or a learned society, but the administrator must also accept the mandate to create overall institutional pride in the conceptual entity - whatever its designation. The most appropriate manner of doing this is to foster the idea that the cause is great. A project such as an outpatient wellness center, a PET facility or a free electron laser program can provide the domain of symbols for a wide constituency which may also give staff members an apparent modicum of control over their personal destinies. Thus, with these special circumstances, the cause has been made just, but, more importantly, staff members have a relation to the cause that they perceive in their personal control.

In the 1930s, there was great emphasis upon the organizational chart in American business and the bureaucratic form of management as championed by Max Weber. Charismatic leadership and innovation were looked upon as conditions that might produce a sprint of productivity, but it was generally held that a detailed and rigid plan would prove more successful over time. Charles Barnard and Elton Mayo at Harvard challenged this emphasis, and in American business we have come to recognize that this type of orientation will not allow us to respond to new initiatives. In medicine, staff members are often more aware of technological innovations, as well as their virtues and limitations, than the administrator. Thus, a responsive administration is the only one that will support the inherent excellence that already exists. Attention to employees - not the organizational chart - will allow the administrator to harness the positive social forces of the department. Medical institutions not so oriented can perpetrate faulty assumptions about this ever-changing discipline for years, despite overwhelming evidence to demonstrate that they are fundamentally incorrect. Several well known medical imaging departments were slow to embrace nuclear medicine in the 1960s and even magnetic resonance in the 1980s due to the "conservatism" of the administration. This posture has proven to be greatly to the detriment of these departments. Change must not only be managed, but should be anticipated, as well.

We are approaching the concept often attributed to the Japanese that an intuitive, informal organization can be managed in a manner which supports excellence. The "Leavitt Diamond" has been revisited and a new more flexible administrative organization is being adopted by those companies in the United States that wish to prosper in the 21st century. Medicine does not have that protracted a duration of time to set our management house in order.

We have learned that more can be accomplished by task forces on specific projects that cross divisional and subspecialty section barriers than by an attempt to manage change utilizing the departmental and often institutional structure. A multivariable administrative framework will allow the medical administrator to enter any project or activity as a participant and not await entry prior to lower-level decisions that might be difficult to modify. The manager will also be seen by the faculty as a participant and not as a gatekeeper, thus giving the staff and, ultimately, the administrator an enhanced sense of pride and self worth. When administrators act as gatekeepers, creativity among faculty is discouraged and conformity in non-innovative areas is encouraged. If faculty and administration are stymied by carpet color selection and furniture dimensions for the area housing the latest in technologic equipment, the value of the facility and added capability may be lost and the realization of its potential greatly compromised.

As the authors of **A Passion for Excellence** note, excellent business enterprises can be defined and described. The more common should include:

1) The ability to learn from those to whom you provide service. Despite the fact that you have work stations on every clinical floor of your hospital and have computerized the film archiving and reporting, your colleague wants to "go over the x-rays with the radiologist."

2) The chance to exercise entrepreneurship, for example, outpatient gallbladder surgery does not exist in your institution. Adding a faculty member with these skills could be expensive. You have been approached with a proposal to attract and fund an individual on the basis that his/her compensation will be determined by performing and charging for this new procedure outside of the traditional partnership context. You now have the responsibility of making this acceptable to the institution.

3) A penchant for action. Certainly, a discipline such as medicine that has seen the introduction of x-ray computed tomography (1974) and magnetic resonance imaging (1982) in the last several decades must have a bias to be responsive to change.

4) Emphasis upon people. To support excellence, one must support those ideals held in greatest regard by one's staff. If the administrator compromises on quality as perceived by his staff, the performance and attitude will mirror their disappointment.

5) Clear agreement and definition of values. The philosophy of an institution is more determinant of its success than space, technology, or even its organizational relationships.

6) Flexible organization with centralism around a select set of core values allows staff to experience both freedom and direction. This focuses the overall purpose of the institution but allows individuals to feel in control of their own destiny.

Some management experts have emphasized the creation of values, but in a discipline with such inherent resources of intellect and leadership, the administrator should also manage the inherent values of the organization. This requires discovery of the collective values of one's employees, analyzing these ideas in the departmental and institutional context, and then articulating these in such a manner that they are understood and accepted by others. Good managers create meanings for their constituency as well as provide them with rewards. Medicine is a service-driven, response discipline, and part of our reward is the appreciation of our fellow physicians for the manner in which we master and utilize our ever-changing, complex and expensive resources. The administrator must provide a leadership role in informing the potential users of these capabilities so that they can appreciate what has been done for them.

Satisfaction of "ownership" for both the technology and the turf can be greatly enhanced by the leadership of the medical manager. The advocacy role in supporting excellence may be the never-ending challenge of the administrator, but its central importance for collective pride should never be underestimated. The manager will approach this responsibility much as a prosecuting attorney should approach pending litigation: marshalling of the facts, documentation of the data, and consideration of the outcomes and techniques of persuasion for a particular line of reasoning. The use of one's staff as "expert witnesses" and to prepare the "brief" will ensure commitment and a sense of purpose and meaning on their part. As an aside, the faculty projected to utilize some future acquisition should be given the primary responsibility for selecting that technology, albeit certainly with the advice and consent of the CEO or chairman. The resource becomes "theirs," and both responsibility for its appropriate use and proper function are virtually assured. Excellence of personnel will be matched by technology.

To return to the initial thesis, the excellence of the medical profession is almost assured by the selection and educational process. The outcome of excellence can be determined and significantly enhanced by the administrator by the creation of an environment that properly supports this excellence.

Chapter 4

A HAPPENING: THE ADMINISTRATOR'S ROLE

The world is comprised of people who:

1) Have no idea of what's happening,
2) Know what is happening but really don't care
3) Make it happen.

How one becomes a member of the latter select few is every administrator's challenge. First you have to develop a desire and a resolve to make a contribution as a manager and then communicate this belief and commitment to those for whom you administrate. You must manage well not simply the status quo but the most rapid rate of change and innovation that can be realistically tolerated in the environment in which you must administrate. In medicine, we have a compelling source for change: technological and information (data) advancement. The skill and craftsmanship involved in appropriately applying technology should in no way obviate the more determinant contribution of the human element. In fact, it is the motivation of people that is the single most crucial element in making whatever it is happen.

Motivation contains a large element of a sense of involvement by those engaged in the performance of tasks that result in the collective progress of the medical institution. The leader must establish an accurate assessment of where the institution is and then formulate a clear direction for the future. This should be presented in an iterative fashion to staff, giving them the opportunity and feeling of involvement. People find it very easy to become enthusiastic about an undertaking if they know what the goal is and how to get there. Through this type of communication you will have captured the hearts and imaginations of those who must execute and deliver in order to make it happen. People inspired to give their best will make it happen and this can be because of your administrative leadership.

Can one first organize and later manage a medical institution to make it happen? Probably, if certain steps are taken. First, the institution should be characterized by openness and the perception of headroom. Headroom is often a feature of the managerial layers in the various units and is also the tolerance that you allow the individual staff members to be wrong. If you and the other administrators can have the staff believe that you act to support rather than control their activities, you have created the idea of headroom.

Another concept that must be embraced by the staff is that they have every right to criticize the administration and management of the institution. However, they should also incur the responsibility of telling the leadership how it should be done. If they do not do this, the exercise will only be complaining and bellyaching - not criticizing. Naysayers can poison an institution, for they neither offer nor participate in any solutions. They are difficult to remove by punishment and disincentives directed their way are often not effective. The best measure to address this issue is to create an environment with enough change and innovation that you deny the naysayers a forum. After a period of time they may join in the progress, but more commonly they will feel estranged from their participating colleagues and seek another venue. Naysayers will not feel welcome for long around a positive, excited group of people. Leopards will not often elect to alter their spots, but they are likely to change their jungle.

After you have identified where you are and have defined your goals, the task of how to get there must be addressed before you can make it happen. The "how to" is a matter of tactics, whether it is Hannibal crossing the Alps, Harold Icahn closing a deal, Louis Nizer selecting a jury, or Howard Baker forging a consensus. The term "tactics" is not meant in a pejorative sense but as the legitimate means to make things happen. The correct tactical decisions by the medical administrator can create a committed determination for what may become a perceived aim. Things happen then because the proper management tactics have forged a resolve that will overcome almost insuperable physical and sometimes fiscal odds. Tactics entail working out the process by which the undertaking will be planned and then balancing the functions that will be necessary to make happen what you wish to happen.

Following a particular tactical course, however, does not mean that you, as the manager, are inexorably committed to it. When it becomes apparent that the consensus of support for what you have selected as the goal or even the methodology chosen to achieve that end is not sufficient for success, reroute your energies and that of your constituency. One of the world's most depressing sights is to see a well-intended leader riding a "dead horse" and admonishing his flock to follow. As leader, take upon yourself both the responsibility for the failure and the plan for redirection.

Making it happen not only involves being first but also being right. Dare to be wrong; and when you recognize that you are, have the grace to redirect and to reroute your constituents as well. Do good while doing well. The race may be won by the swift, but their travel must be in the right direction. Unquestionably, because of the independence and education among the medical constituency, those in the trenches need to have a common goal for the group to succeed.

Progress is really the saga of change, and those who create progress know how to manage change. Change must be perceived as opportunity, emphasizing the benefits but not denying the risks. One's staff must be made to feel comfortable with change. Preserving the status quo is momentarily the most comfortable posture for human beings. However, over the course of time it is the highest risk strategy one can adopt because change is inevitable. In medicine, the introduction of new treatments, technology, and regulation absolutely ensures that we are most definitely about the management of change. You not only make it happen but must be prepared to manage the "happening." Before you introduce new technology, you must also have the consensus of your constituency that this is important and that it represents an appropriate allocation of their resources. Inducing change may require one set of administrative skills, but managing it requires another.

Change often brings about anxiety. For many, it is the embodiment of uncertainty and can be unsettling. To manage change and to make it happen, you must address this anticipated reaction among your personnel. At the time you are inducing change, you must also evidence compassion - not so much in the paternalistic sense but as a genuine expression of respect for the concerns and anxieties of those you manage. You do not want to remove their self-reliance, because this will be needed to sustain the change and to make it happen.

I can recall the first introduction of an electronic method of patient identification and scheduling in our institution. We had several individuals at the reception desk who had been employed there for over 20 years and were in their late fifties, while I was the young knight who had arrived several years before to lead them into the 21st century. To these loyal employees, a CRT was the invention of the devil, and they were concerned that they would never be able to use it. They were not convinced that this new technology was better than the manual method they had employed for decades. To make it happen, I knew this would take more than a motivational speech of leader to employee; instead, I tried to convey my own concerns. I told them that I also had no computer literacy and that microwave ovens and VCRs were anxiety hurdles for me. However, I was going to give this a try because it was supposed to make us more efficient and able to serve our patients better. The goal was now to learn to work the machine, and the CEO had expressed the same anxiety and skepticism as the affected employees had but also gave them a reason for "giving it a try." We had gone from "you make it work or else" to "let's see if it will work."

Common concerns can truly breed loyalty and, interestingly, confidence that by working together some very challenging objectives can be met. People make things happen, and if their concerns and anxieties are not appreciated in a nurturing manner then they will not believe that the objective represents a common purpose and may challenge the judgement that the goal represents a common benefit. Making it happen means causing people to want it to happen.

A very basic human trait is the desire to do better. In the United States, there are several huge industries based on this concept - from improving one's physical condition, to self motivation, to cosmetic surgery. The marketing strategy in each of these is to make the public feel that this is something they need in order to be and to do better. To make it happen, the need has to be felt to the extent that the effort to achieve this end becomes only a matter of strategy. Wishing to make it happen is now a given, and how to make happen is the goal.

People who make it happen were not necessarily born that way nor is this an entirely learned behavior pattern. Personality is most probably an admixture of congenital basic traits modified by early life experience. "People skills" are largely acquired through our experience and social interaction. Because of these characteristics, the earth is populated by a fairly large cadre of people who, under the appropriate circumstances, can make things happen. Medical administrators come from varied backgrounds and evidence almost a complete spectrum of personal behavior — some of which is adaptive. They all have certain common characteristics, such as desire and the ability to identify a goal and articulate it to others. Between the desire and the goal, there is a required amount of activity and goal-directed effort. To experience a happening is a pleasure. To make a happening is a joy.

Chapter 5

SUCCESSFUL MANAGEMENT

A great deal has been written about management principles as they apply to medicine. Responsibility for increasing employee performance is one of the most critical concerns as we in medicine attempt to do more with less. Managers in the health care field who empower employees to higher levels of performance will be indispensable; those who fail will not.

There is a common thread found in such indispensable managers (whether in business, the medical profession, leading armies or coaching athletic teams), a conceptual model for the aspirant to follow, and specific habits that can be duplicated.

Management studies show that successful managers are similar, and close observation discloses several particular qualities that appear common. They are all goal-driven, have good communication skills, continually empower and inspire their staff and employees, act with a caring attitude, and embody a total commitment to the responsibility of the organization. These qualities have become the personal habits of most indispensable managers. Since habits are acquired behaviors, they can, in theory, be adopted by others on the staff or in the organization. However, all of this requires an expressed desire coupled with an appropriate investment of time, energy, and patience.

One should categorize needs into different levels of priority, and understanding those levels, as well as those of employees, is vital. Abraham Maslow noted this in "Hierarchy of Needs." He opined that the priorities are first, food and shelter; second, safety and security; third, belonging, friendship, and love; fourth, self-esteem, status, and ego; fifth, self-actualization and self-fulfillment. The concepts are based on the idea that people naturally attempt to satisfy lower needs before moving to higher levels.

As the administrator, assessing your position in this hierarchy is useful to motivating yourself, then your employees, to higher levels of excellence. Initially, the first step is to be aware of your needs, giving clarity to your personal agenda, and then those of your medical staff. The level at which employees are currently performing provides an understanding of their personal agendas, just as your performance reflects yours. The goal is targeting all motivational efforts at each individual's personal agenda, thus assuring a genuine commitment to the common goal of the institution.

Fredrick Herzberg, a social scientist of the '50s and '60s, challenged the common perceptions of motivation. He labeled a number of commonly regarded motivators such as salary, working conditions, and company policies as "hygiene factors," indicating that they are important for morale but had little relevance in motivating high-level performance. Herzberg's work is one of the more commonly applied management principles today, though apparently little recognized in the field of health care.

Indispensable medical administrators know their personal agenda and have developed a system to convert this to a more general context. They then develop success habits that support their system, and transfer this to their medical staff as well. As a child models behaviors of parents and a mentee of a mentor, staff will follow a good manager model. In the lean, downsizing business environment of the '90s, managers in business, and in the medical business will be challenged to accomplish more with fewer resources at their disposal. Habits must be developed that conserve resources. Any behavior repeated regularly develops into a habit, and behavioral psychologists agree that this process requires as little as three weeks. Thus, in theory, an ideal manager, in just the proper environment, could actuate or motivate their constituency for a carefully articulated activity in less than a month.

What are these patterns of behavior that should be employed by the medical administrator? It should be emphasized that the characteristics of the manager are the determinative factors. Indispensable managers are usually result-oriented. They have goals, subgoals, and corresponding fixed activities for most actions. Aspirations, results, and rewards are evident in their activities. These people instinctively tune into Maslow's hierarchal levels themselves and into those they set out to motivate. The strongest leaders have the most clearly defined mission, and their motivation is self-motivation.

Managers cannot always motivate another person to achieve. They can, however, create an environment that stimulates self-motivation. In the office, this is an environment where employees commit to result-oriented, time-specific goals that support institutional goals. "Goals are the prerequisite to achievement," according to Louis Scott. "The astute leader helps people set goals compatible to those of their organization and then provides the tools for achievement." A manager can create a goal-driven environment by making certain everyone is aware of corporate, division, and department annual goals. A manager can visit with every employee and assist them to establish personal goals, but in a medical environment this may be impractical. They can use Maslow's hierarchy levels as the basis for appealing to each employee's need level and by knowing the exact activity or work requirements of each person and motivating them to invest into a performance level, thus giving them the opportunity to establish their own goals.

A good medical manager will prosper by being realistic but aggressive; not everyone will perform at his or her potential. For group activities, use the "buddy" system. Working partners, peer supporting peer, can create extraordinary chemistry. By describing goals into monthly, weekly, and daily activities, they do not appear overwhelming, as individual activity is not. Activity often drives goals.

Every member of the team, from the receptionist at the waiting room desk to the most senior physician, must be goal-focused and should employ the manager's system in their routine activities. This is not easy, because there are no shortcuts in the communication process. Each member of the staff needs to be continuously informed. High-level communication is required, and this requires time, energy, and creativity; it goes beyond the spoken word and often requires a working understanding of metaphors, role models, images, and symbols. Metaphors can serve as powerful devices in communicating goals and other vital system-related information.

Rewards both communicate and symbolize some level of accomplishment toward the ultimate objective in a medical environment. In employing symbolic rewards, a manager should be mindful of several considerations, such as the current need level of an employee and a reward that fosters ongoing motivation. Despite the importance of metaphors and symbolic rewards, the most powerful medium is the manager's spoken word. One-on-one communication, followed with supportive action, will motivate almost anyone. Newsletters and bulletin boards are excellent support devices but will be treated with quiet contempt if the manager's personal touch does not accompany it. Personal praise has proved without a doubt to be the best motivator of any group of employees, including those in health care. "The heart of the fool is in his mouth, but the mouth of the wise is in his heart," said Benjamin Franklin more than 200 years ago. Recognition and praise motivate people closer to their potential than tangibles. Discipline physicians and other employees privately to keep ego and self-esteem intact. Remember to praise, recognize, and praise! The manager serves as a role model for the institution. One technique to ensure this lasting quality is to write letters to employees for special accomplishments; they will be reread, and this may, in fact, re-motivate.

A good manager should effect positive energy transference. This is not to be confused with the off-touted quality of charisma, implying that either you have it or you do not, which is not true. Every manager should master the facility of transferring positive energy to others. This is empowerment. It evokes the best in others and is a motivational technique that can be acquired. Everyone has a dream, including staff, whose aspirations may reside deep within their personal agendas. Indispensable managers uncover these individual ambitions and connect a relationship to institutional goals, and communicate this process to the staff.

After establishing an employee's dream, the manager should build a bridge to the corporate mission. Staff will go to all types of extremes if they can believe in themselves, their aspirations, and their medical institution. A Latin proverb says, "He can who believes he can." That same message is voiced by many of today's business leaders. To be successful as medical managers, we have to help people believe in themselves and recognize their talents. Find out what each employee's aspirations are and communicate these into goals that connect to institutional goals. The medical manager may break down individual goals for their staff into daily activities and foster team belief among the staff through meetings and hold employees accountable to goals and activities. One should thus expect employees to believe and achieve.

There is an old adage, "People don't care how much you know until they know how much you care." Profound in its simplicity, the applications of these concepts in the medical enterprize are boundless. A personal bond created by caring is easily accomplished because humans crave support. Caring is an extension of communication and empowerment, and it involves action and words. Ross Perot empowered people to invest tremendous amounts of time in building his business and gained the total support of their families. The bond that he developed with his original team came to be worth billions of dollars.

As a manager, demonstrate caring by giving your undivided attention when people speak. Follow through with your pronouncements. Understand the needs and wants of family members of staff. Remember that small things mean everything. As a successful manager, you must be totally committed. This is what provides focus to one's mission. Indispensable managers lead people to higher levels by targeted actions applied consistently to all staff members. Commitment sometimes means listening to an employee when you might rather be doing something else, or repeating, for the fifth time, a key component of your medical philosophy as it relates to your overall institutional plan, until it is understood and can be acted upon. Medicine is a very complicated discipline, and repetition can be very useful.

Indispensable management is a mind-set, an inner game exercised by every super-achiever who leads. The willingness and methodology to grow, to become personally involved, to invest time and money, and to be focused on a goal are not taught in most business schools and no medical schools. However, they are the ingredients of successful management in any environment. Therefore, before any change occurs, commitment, coupled with an action plan, is the initial step. To achieve this, the manager should focus all efforts on the mission as defined and then lead by example with integrity and a strong work ethic. As the manager you must deliver on promises, regardless of how small. Your integrity is at stake and is assessed by observation of your activity or the perception of your effort.

Management success habits are nondiscriminating, and any willing manager can develop these qualities into habits. Once the inculcation of these traits is achieved, the newly acquired habits will serve as a model for others in the institution. Begin this process with yourself. You are the person who is going to become an indispensable manager. As you develop into this conceptual model, you will refine your system of management and your staff will transform themselves into your indispensable team.

Chapter 6

PLAY THE HAND YOU ARE DEALT

Among the least effective methods of management is that of waiting for all the resources necessary before initiating the activity to achieve a particular goal you have. Most people in this world, including physicians, are waiting for something to happen, whether that "something" is a new technology, additional space in the institution, or even inspiration and some ethereal divine guidance to truly initiate some process. For most people by operating in this mode, "it" never happens and they simply cannot understand why.

As an administrator, it is unquestionably prudent to acquire as many resources as you need to discharge your responsibilities. However, you should be mindful that the resources you are allowed to acquire oftentimes requires some institutional financial risk and may, if an extremely new innovation or for example a prototype instrument, be acquired as "an article of faith." You should also bear in mind that we all have someone judging our performance; with the institutional administration, they may be judging by *only* the infamous "bottom line" and not the parameters you prefer, such as quality of care. If the administration fails to respond to your various entreaties "proving" the need for a particular acquisition, rather than cease and desist, see if you have an alternative or if you have another hand to play in this process. For example, the institution may not be convinced of the proposed action by your computer-generated financial drafts or the break even analysis which your resident MBA has prepared for you, possibly using the newly described "voodoo economics." On the other hand, the institutional leadership may well be persuaded by your clinicians who can translate "down time" into quality of patient care terms; this is equivalent to providing yourself another hand and one you have dealt yourself. In the interim, use the technology you have been given while documenting the effect of its inadequacy in such terms as down time, image quality, and repeat studies. This is the hand you have been dealt, so use it to fashion a subsequent "better" submission.

Once, in the late 1970s, we were denied the opportunity to have some newly developed digital radiographic equipment. This technology was relatively unproven, denying us a convincing pro forma analysis. Our clinical colleagues were satisfied with the alternative methodology for these studies, leaving us without a constituency there. Even within our own department, there was no particularly overwhelming consensus that this was an essential capability. Our institution was unconvinced. However, we still had resources to offer in this acquisition process; our "hand" was the expertise of our staff in evaluation of technology. Through a series of exploratory discussions, we learned that the manufacturer had failed to convince many (if any) institutions to acquire this digital equipment in a traditional lease or purchase arrangement, largely for the same reasons we had been denied by our parent institution. Additionally, we were made aware that a very large hospital management company planned to consider purchasing a significant number of the instruments but, to date, had not done so, due to these same uncertainties. The hospital management company was reluctant to make such an important financial commitment on data largely generated in the manufacturing plant of the instrument company.

We approached both parties, playing the hand of our scientific expertise to forge an arrangement by which we would be given the equipment, evaluate its performance in our hospital setting using our criteria, and be compensated for this activity by the hospital management company. At the conclusion of this arrangement, the medical equipment company received a detailed report of the instrumentation suggesting some modifications, the health care management company received a presumably unbiased report of the virtues and limitations of the equipment and recommendations regarding its appropriate distribution in the facilities they managed. We were able to acquire and use this prototype equipment and were compensated for the hand we played, that of scientific and clinical expertise.

Concerned about conflict of interest, we studiously avoided any advocacy role (marketing is an inappropriate "hand" for a professional group) and steadfastly refused to draw comparisons of instrumentation by different vendors for external use (also not a proper hand in most circumstances). We played the hand we had: clinicians, scientists, space, and an entity (the Vanderbilt Center for Medical Imaging Research) designed to participate in this type of activity. Certain resources had been created at the behest of our parent institution, and they received the benefit of the instrumentation.

Often, avoidance of an activity is as great or is a greater administrative challenge than participation. You may not have the "hand" you thought you had. This may require a very critical assessment of one's assets and skills related to the anticipated endeavor, and then a reasoned decline of the opportunity may have to be provided. In the latter task, the administrator may need to inform their constituency that they do not possess a particular capacity or skill that your employees believe or believed they have.

When we were exploring alternative methods to finance an elaborate PET/cyclotron facility, one posed to us was to manufacture unique radiopharmaceuticals and sell them to other users for profit. Several consultants provided us with rather imaginative and enthusiastic data regarding our potential income. However, as we reviewed the practical aspects of this undertaking, it became clear that expertise in marketing and distribution were absolutely crucial for financial success of this activity. These were not skills that we possessed with our present group of clinicians/scientists and thus, in reality, a hand we did not have nor were likely to acquire. Our talents were in garnering extramural funding through grant submissions, and we best apply our energies there, which was the course we chose.

Playing the hand you have been dealt may possibly sound fundamentally naive, even trite. As an expression, it may even possess a frivolous ring, but the concept has important administrative substance. This management technigue will allow the medical institution to emphasize its strengths and engage primarily in those undertakings in which the opportunity for success is greatest. It will also allow one to achieve success incrementally, which may be the only viable avenue. To await all of the resources necessary to achieve a particular goal will often place one in administrative rigor mortis and deny the opportunity for short-term goals leading to the long-term success. Rarely is one dealt a "royal flush," but creative use of the resources at the administrator's disposal may still achieve the overall equivalent of a grand slam. Continued small steps in a positive direction will enlist the enthusiasm of one's constituency and often the compassion of the controller of the resources. Opportunities can be lost by failure to play the hand you have been dealt.

Chapter 7

THE ISSUE OF CONTROL

The administration of each discipline has a unique ethos that can characterize the human relationships intrinsic to that profession. Medicine is certainly no exception. A common trait among leaders in all fields is that they have an intense desire to feel that they have the proper measure of control; control of the means to effect solutions for the responsibilities they have and some measure of control of their own destiny. The discipline of medicine has inherent complexities and natural administrative arrangements that make it very difficult to accommodate a feeling of control. The level, intensity, and, all too often, character of the service is determined by others. Requests for services are often generated by clinical colleagues each having a particular style and mode of seeking consultation. The administrative leader must not only adapt to the spectrum of behavior manifest by the staff but must respond to changes in the level of service demands.

Sometimes the service element incumbent upon the medical institution exceeds the resources available to a willing administrator. The administrator either attempts to acquire these resources or can attempt to negotiate acceptance of not providing the service; each of these options is a particularly formidable task. In order to acquire the additional resources which often are institutional, the temporal character of the solution may be out of phase with the demand; the demand being acute and the institutional response time protracted.

In certain areas of medicine the administrator has far more alternatives of response than in others. For example, the radiology chairman has no acceptable choice when the institution is unable to replace or refurbish a CT scanner that is obsolete and its "downtime" has become unacceptable. The administrator in a "real-time" service department will gain little compassion in explaining to the clinical staff that studies cannot be performed in the timely fashion they expect due to an institutional decision regarding equipment that resulted in the instrumentation not being replaced or even repaired after it has far excluded its original projected half life.

The medical administrator often feels controlled from below by the demand creating a responsibility and controlled from above by the institutional hierarchy that is in charge of the allocation of those resources the administrator needs in order to respond to the demands. We are dealing with ill human beings cared for by concerned, articulate and aggressive medical advocates who do not have the luxury of time or the ambiance of emotional detachment to formulate and negotiate an acceptable response. From the viewpoint of hospital and medical center administration, the request from the specialty director is viewed in a compassionate but somewhat detached manner. After all, their immediate fate will suffer little if the clinical demand is not met or not responded to appropriately for a "reasonable" period of time. However, if the Board of Trust of the institution or the university comptroller recognizes a disparity between a large, visible capital expenditure and the income stream, then the administrators become at risk. The chairman sometimes has little or no influence on their sense of urgency nor can he control their priorities.

The medical administrator must accept a certain amount of external control as a fact and attempt to elicit the assistance of the demand group to secure the resources from those who are truly in control. This method of administration should be perceived as giving control to gain control — it probably does not conform to the image that the administrator/chair anticipated early in their careers or was prepared to project when they were first placed in charge of the department; naivete almost always distorts reality.

I remember a personal experience that I had in the mid-1970s. A person whom I admired very much had just resigned as chair of what we all believed was a very successful department in a good medical school. What made it so difficult to reconcile was that this chairman was at the same time president of several national organizations and chairman of the board of his college discipline. He held commissions and offices making him one of the most powerful people in his specialty. Feeling that some great tragedy had befallen him, I thought I best avoid whatever it was, so I asked him why he gave up this highly compensated, powerful position. He gave a very succinct and memorable answer "I realized that I was being given more and more (responsibility) and was in control of less and less. When my control got below 10%, I quit".

Several days later I was still attempting to reconcile my aspirations and expectations with this disturbing revelation and went to see my mentor, Russell Morgan, who by then was Dean of the Johns Hopkins Medical School. I spoke to him about this issue of control and if you wanted to avoid being controlled should you then move from department chairman, to dean to vice chancellor for health affairs to... By the time I finished the question the answer was apparent — you never escape control but you can understand it, modify it at times and learn to accommodate it. Dr. Morgan opined "if you do not take the power too seriously you can handle the control better. The two things you can exert the greatest control over are your research and your publications. If you do these to your satisfaction, then no one is in control of you. That is where most administrators lose their frame of reference."

Since that helpful insight, I believe I have discovered another. As an administrator those people you choose to assist with their careers provide you with the response and satisfaction that give you a feeling of control because you may have made initial choices for them.

Medical administrators must accept the fact that certain disciplines are a service specialty and, therefore, a demand/response one. Leaders in these disciplines can exercise only a limited amount of control over the demand and are not often in complete control of the resources to respond to the demand. In order to acquire these resources they must appeal for these resources from others. After having done this,they will sometimes still not be successful in meeting the demand through no fault of their own. This is the nature of service disciplines and the realistic circumstance in which we function. However, there accrue significant benefits to belonging to this discipline; the improvements and innovations offer unlimited opportunities for personal enjoyment, intellectual growth, and the chance to make a contribution.

How you perceive control and what you as an administrator do with it will most often determine your accommodation and your personal satisfaction with your management position. Control is either a myth or a mirage and since one can never attain it, select some other focus to emphasize your administrative accomplishments. There are many policy issues that affect this concept or control through mechanisms such as RVSs to reward "cognitive medical care" or DRGs (diagnosis related groups) to limit overall expenditures related to health care delivery. More and more "managed" care will erode the administrative concept of control.

Control or the perception of control is a very basic human concern especially for someone as aggressive and independent as most department chairmen. It must be viewed in perspective, however, and control must not be equated with success.

Chapter 8

A CHOICE OF DURATION AND KEEPING IT REALISTIC

The rapid turnover in administrative personnel in the health care field has been ascribed to many etiologies. At present, the half-life of medical school deans, vice presidents or vice chancellors, and certain chairs is unacceptably short, resulting in so many vacancies that many departments and institutions are literally adrift. Search committees, in recognition of this phenomenon, appear to be selecting individuals whose primary virtue is that they appear stable, experienced, and predictable. Candidates who are particularly aggressive, imaginative, and unpredictable seem to be avoided as an unacceptable risk. Private medical groups also seem to be adopting this same posture, which is not unreasonable, for at no time in its modern history has the practice of medicine been beset with so many uncertainties and external as well as internal variables as today. These range from such present factors as ICD-9 coding, voluntary assignment, caps on equipment spending, FDA approval of new procedures, and malpractice concerns to impending ones such as the application of relative value scales (RVS) in practice and the "doom" of health care reform.

For certain disciplines in medicine, it has been said that patients demand the best of both worlds: the diagnostic precision of the latest in biomedical imaging technology delivered by an individual with the compassion, understanding and time of the traditional family practitioner. David Rogers, the former head of the Robert Wood Johnson Foundation, has been quoted in a July 31, 1989 article of *Time*: "Technology forms a great moat between the patient and the physician." In a service specialty, physicians must respond to two constituencies: the public on the demand side and the administration under which they labor on the supply side. Given the number of simultaneous challenges, it is little wonder that life in these leadership roles is traumatic and unacceptably short. However, one technique that seems to be extremely helpful in providing a measure of satisfaction that, in itself, is sustaining; this is the deliberate separation of one's goals and the responses thereto into short, intermediate, and long-term expectations.

In order to provide this differentiation of rewards to goals and efforts, the manager must analyze both the demands and the resources necessary to appropriately respond to these perceived or defined responsibilities. As an example, the demand for rapid information retrieval may be urgent on the part of one's clinical colleagues, but the overall solution in the form of automation and installation of a picture archiving and communicating system (PACS) will require time and the acquisition of significant resources by a rather lengthy and unpredictable institutional budgetary process. The department is doomed to disfavor, disavowal, and apparent defeat if the appropriate length of response time is not recognized by all. Once this is done, there is now the possibility of interim measures that can alleviate some of the emotional content of the problem. The "pie" may be acquired by the slice not the dish.

Alternatively, a problem such as ICD-9 coding has a required response time and a due date. The administrator must recognize this, quickly analyze the present and needed resources, and then set forth in an expeditious manner to respond. In this circumstance, the manager must recognize that the determination of the appropriate response may require several iterations, and flexibility and mobility are not manifestations of administrative error but evidence of a perceived mandate subject to redefinition without the necessity of ascribing guilt or blame.

When a particular proposal or problem from either the staff or the institution is brought to the administrator should try very hard to assess a realistic time in which this can be resolved or achieved. So much of the personal sense of accomplishment, achievement, and satisfaction depends upon this being an accurate assessment that one should accord this prediction of resources and time an extremely high priority. In this manner, the administration should not contribute to my own dissatisfaction and can act as an effective counsel to the staff. After all "Rome wasn't..., Mt. Everest was scaled in one..., the Empire State Building (or Sears Tower) was fashioned...and Henry Aaron's RBI's were not all the result of grand slams.

Chapter 9

IN PERSPECTIVE

One's administrative technique is often characterized by others in superlatives. When we are made aware of these descriptions, more often than not we are disappointed that we are not perceived by others as we think of ourselves. Our style, attitude, and modus operandi are often viewed in much narrower and focused terms than we believe fair and accurate. This disparity between our self-concept and the opinion of others may represent an administrative problem itself or be the manifestation of one.

In medicine, the half-life of a medical administrator is among the shortest in American business. Conventional wisdom has reasoned that this is due to the demands of administrating an industrial complex requiring techniques for which we have not had sufficient preparation and, concommitantly, removing the manager from the fundaental doctor/patient relationship. The administrator's responsibilities do often remove them from the clinical service where they have received their previous rewards; in fact, their achievements in the clinical arena may have been responsible for their promotion to their present administrative post. To now be denied access to the clinic because of administrative demands may be viewed as a frustrating circumstance.

These reasons significantly contribute to the failure of many administrators, but another factor that is equally compelling and possibly even more pervasive is the failure to view the needs of staff and colleagues in an institutional perspective.

For those of us who have been administrators during a time of great institutional growth or of a specific mandate favorably directed at our goals, all of our administrative techniques and style appear to have resulted in success. However, even in this circumstance, geometric expansion and unabated growth cannot continue forever. At some time, the medical institution will become large enough to raise concerns about whether or not the size and importance of our activity are appropriate for the general good. When this occurs, the medical administrator will need to view the competing issues in perspective and will need to evidence the posture of an institutional manager. Every wish or demand cannot be presented as the highest priority. Every turf issue, while undeniably important, cannot be approached as a struggle to avoid instant annihilation. All victories do not have to be 100%; some may be acceptable at 51%.

Historically, a general administrative tenet has been that the manager cannot effectively negotiate unless he is prepared to "put his position on the line." This form of edge-hanging politics requires very little judgement but on a daily basis is hardly effective. More reasonably, the administrator has to decide what is important both for the institution and the public, weigh these to determine the relative priorities, and then act as the leader of a constituency which has competing demands that exceed limited resources. The leadership must be viewed as one that perceives needs and resources in perspective.

Sometimes an individual administrator may be viewed as aggressive, forceful, or bold; however, over the course of time, a leader seen as reasonable and a member of the institutional team will be most successful in the complex medical entities. Managers should make a conscious effort to be consistent and straightforward, in order to be perceived by others in the same manner as they view themselves.

Chapter 10

PROXIMITY: GEOGRAPHIC AND PERCEPTIVE

Progress in medicine has largely become a collaborative and cooperative endeavor. Those successful in both funding and output have seemed to develop an environment that maximizes the interactive opportunities. Are these techniques of circumstance amenable to management or do they occur more as a result of chance than by design? Certainly, each may contribute.

One is reminded of the philosophy of the late Vince Lombardi ("You make your breaks") and the equally applicable Thomas Alva Edison quote of what his success was due to. What may appear as chance might well be due to clever strategic planning. For example, certain specialties should transcend the usual collaborative arrangements and involve the more traditional undergraduate specialties of physics, engineering and biomedical engineering. Thus, the basic science faculty of the medical school, essential for certain kinds of intellectual endeavors, many not represent appropriate substitutes for collaboration.

The location of one's department on a university campus affords the most effective arrangement wherein the collaborative agreements can be arranged. Alternatively, physical dislocation often does not allow the meaningful intellectual interchange necessary for productive research. Thus, geography is important, and when it is present it should be effectively utilized. When it is absent, it should be appropriately accounted for in any protocol or set of outcome expectations. As a personal example, our initial magnetic resonance research was with the chemistry department, microwave attenuation with biomedical engineering, digital radiology with computer sciences, and free electron laser work with physics in our parent university. All of these disciplines were physically located adjacent to the medical school on the university campus.

A legendary real estate magnate once noted that the three most determinative characteristics of the value of a property are "location, location, and location." While one might pose that this is equally important in collaborative research, plowing the field of uncharted medical knowledge is more complicated and, hopefully, more important than real estate. Placing scholars in close physical proximity does not ensure that they will be together in an intellectual sense; it tends to maximize the opportunity but does require efforts in "designed chance."

Technology is exciting, but it can also be intimidating; anything unknown or partially understood often evokes a defensive or skeptical reaction. To promote an appreciation of the resources offered by technology again requires an effort to achieve proximity, but in this instance it is intellectual proximity. Mutual respect among scientists is not fostered by guarding the information of one's technology but in sharing it, explaining it, and managing it to achieve a closer intellectual proximity. For example, the MRS and ESR communities felt initially that the owners and purveyors of the MRI technology were suspect; after all, "those gadgets cost over a million dollars, enough money to fund our research for a decade." However, when the virtues of combining imaging data with spectroscopic measurements came to their mutual awareness and the potential collaborators learned the virtues, limitations, and engineering principles employed in these unique instruments, enthusiasm for collaborative research grew rapidly. Their educational process was a designed effort not left to chance but might have been interpreted as such. If this was the case, then the design was an especially effective one, for it achieved the desired goal without appearing to coerce, regiment, or be the result of marketing—all anathemas to independent-minded scientists.

The infrastructure required to discharge the clinical responsibilities of certain disciplines fashions an environment in which scholarly proximity is inherent and can be easily created. An example is a cyclotron/PET facility. To produce the short-lived isotopes, prepare the radiopharmaceuticals, create the appropriate imaging protocols, deliver the correct medical interpretation, and determine the appropriate therapeutic inferences requires a team of scientists. This complicated but organized team will very likely be comprised of a physicist, engineer, radiochemist, radiopharmacologist, specially trained technologists, and a complement of MDs (usually a neuroradiologist and a nuclear cardiologist, but there may be other subspecialties represented). By preparing staffing patterns to accommodate the anticipated clinical responsibility, one unwittingly produces a team of people who are certainly in creative proximity and are quite likely to share a perceived common destiny. By management of this closeness, one assists in perpetuating the chance of mutual goals among the contributors.

This chapter has discussed those circumstances in which geographical proximity is rather comfortably achieved, but there are other situations where it is essential to have an effective collaboration, though this may be quite difficult to fashion. In my experience of an academic setting, advising and supervising graduate students in other disciplines is an endeavor that is mutually beneficial to the involved departments and to the graduate students. However, the courtship and marriage must be very carefully orchestrated. First, one's resources must be made known to the basic science department by lectures, seminars, or demonstrations. The students should be attracted to do research in a department because of its recognized resources or because of a particular thesis project that they have agreed upon with their advisor. Medical institutions should never be cast in the perceived role of raiding or active recruiting of graduate students from the basic scientists. One must be very attentive to the feelings of basic science colleagues and not be guided solely by your own personal opinion of their actions. There is a marvelous opportunity for collaboration, but the feelings of the basic science department must be respected.

Can these thoughts and management approaches be utilized in other activities of a medical institution? They probably can, but the external demands of clinical responsibility have a greater inherent tendency for cooperation and inducement for collaborative behavior than independent research does. Independent research will be truly independent unless certain positive measures are taken. While academic survival may well be viewed as an issue in only one area of a department, is this an acute issue? The bringing together of people to conduct meaningful research is both a challenge and an opportunity.

Chapter 11

A QUESTION OF FAIRNESS

The standard interview with the CEO of any business, whether it is a multinational corporation, an industrial giant, a successful venture capital enterprise, or a medical institution, will almost always include the revelations "I'm tough but I am fair," "I demand but I reward in an equitable manner," and "if you produce you receive." The necessity of such statements suggests that a major issue in any organization is the perception of fairness by the participants and the image of equity by prospective employees or, in the case of a medical instriction, staff or faculty.

Although there are many business characteristics in the health care industry, the application of traditional industry management techniques and extrapolation of business compensation schemes are often problematic. While exclusive contracts and the application of antitrust legislation to our particular discipline has many parallels in the business sector, there are complexities in medicine that make the issue of fairness almost unique and the challenge of the administrative chief a particularly difficult one. This is especially relevant in medical teaching institutions if it adds the responsibilities of teacher and researcher to the income producing activity of delivery of clinical service.

Equity is not difficult to achieve in a business in which the measurement of performance is easily quantified since the task is not divided into markedly disparate subunits. If the workers produce widgets, a simple total of the number of widgets per unit time will rather accurately determine productivity. If the widgets are the same size, configuration, and constructed in the same manner, then the measurement is even less difficult. In this circumstance also, the differences in training, skill, and expectations of the workers would be minimized. If they were satisfied with repetitively producing a simple object, their demands for special arrangements of compensation and reward would probably be few.

The CEO of a medical unit has an entirely different environment in which to administrate. The staff will, through the selection process, consist of a group of overachievers, often demanding and highly motivated, who possess at least one and sometimes several postgraduate degrees. These staff members, by virtue of their innate intelligence and training, will possess rare, if not unique, skills which are in great demand.

Because of the development of new technologies and improvements in instrumentation in medicine, new specialties and subspecialties have been created so rapidly that a cadre of physicians and technologists have not been trained in sufficient numbers to fill certain of the positions that do and potentially exist. Recruitment, as well as retention, of these physicians has produced arrangements that have created significant real and perceived inequities in these departments. The faculty might be regarded as the medical equivalent of the "bonus babies" of baseball or the "free agents" of the NFL. While the CEO of the medical group may be quite comfortable with this compensation differential because it may be the only method whereby service will be provided and the image of the institution enhanced, the other members of the team who have been "toiling in the vineyards" may not agree that the sacrifice for the benefit of the whole is appropriate or fair.

Attempting to standardize and quantify work units in medicine is fraught with considerable hazard. Third-party payors and other compensation schemes have made the calculation of equitable financial reward in medicine very complex. For instance, can one quantify a supraselective angiogram, a drainage procedure under CT guidance or a colonoscopy with 10...20...30 chest radiographs or 2...3...7 barium enemas? The answer is obvious, but we do not want to leave those in charge of the relative value scale (RVS) concept to do this calculation for us.

The institutional image is often best projected by some of the more dramatic subspecialties. Therefore, should staff in these subspecialties receive greater compensation than faculty working in more "routine" areas? Most marketing types would answer in the affirmative. When considered from this marketing perspective, fairness is almost impossible for the medical administrator to determine and much more difficult for the other members of theinstitution to accept.

Thus far, this communication has considered only the evaluation of the discharge of clinical service by the CEO and the difficult question of fairness. In an academic institution, this circumstance is greatly complicated by the additional faculty responsibility of teaching and research. The quality of research is difficult to measure, but funding levels and acceptance of publications in highly refereed journals provides some rather vague and oblique guidelines. The judgment balance between quantity of publications and quality is very problematical for the CEO in deciding about resource allocations to faculty. Evaluation of teaching is, at best, an imprecise science. Judging the effectiveness in teaching is often the reflection of an opinion of performance and is quite subjective. The CEO probably has little data from personal observation to render a fair assessment of this activity.

When the three mandates of clinical service, teaching, and research are viewed in the conglomerate, it is difficult for the medical CEO to weigh these fairly. Teaching, which is less quantifiable, is often underemphasized. Even though research may be the predominant interest of the academic CEO/chairperson, the medical center administration is much more likely to be vitally interested in and emphasize the income generated through clinical service for financial viability. Thus, this parameter has very high priority as a survival reality. This will easily offset lack of honors for teaching excellence or even a shortfall in research funds. For the administrative leader of the medical facility, personal inclinations should be valued in relation to the welfare and policies of the entire institution. Individual departmental choices may reflect the CEO's interpretation of the desires of the medical center leadership and occasionally will demonstrate some disparity with the wishes of the department members.

From this lengthy characterization of the circumstance of medical institutions and the milieu in which the CEO/chairperson/administrator operates, the issue of fairness as perceived by the staff is obviously an extremely important one. The administrator would wish to always be fair but, more importantly, would always hope to be perceived by others as fair. The creation of this perception may depend as much upon style as substance. For example, to have every major decision within the institution arrived upon by vote of all the members is a blueprint for indecision and chaos. It obviates the leadership of the CEO, except to influence votes by persuasion, and is an inherently inefficient process. To attempt some involved formula that would mathematically grade clinical effort to arrive at a "fair" method of compensation soon becomes unduly complex and weighing factors are never unanimously agreed upon. The CEO cannot escape into some highly regularized method of reward that is far more available to the administrative leadership in the business world.

To project the image of fairness the CEO no matter what profession, must be decisive. Indecisiveness and requiring an inappropriate time to render a decision will result in employee distrust and frustration. After a timely decision has been rendered, the reasons for the decision should be appropriately shared with the affected staff. These steps in the decision process should be presented in a logical fashion as data, not as concepts to be accepted or denied. Once the staff is informed of the reasoning process, they are more likely to accept a decision as fair even though they may not agree with the decision itself.

Most staff members in medical institutions have compassion for the complexities of the leader's position and are predisposed to judge any reasoned decision as "fair." In dealing with such a highly educated, intelligent constituency, discussing the virtues and alternatives for any decision is very helpful in having them judge it as "fair." Explanation of the implications of another decision will add greatly to the "rightness" of the one made. However, the administrator should be mindful that "fair" is not always the equivalent of "right" or "correct;" and the decision should, however, approach "honest."

In the complex environment of a medical institution, the administrator will be remarkably effective if judged as "fair" by the staff as well as by colleagues outside the department in other disciplines. There is no absolute formula to achieve this characterization, but decisiveness and candor are extremely helpful. If administrators can project the image of an honest attempt to wrestle with the issue of fairness, they will be successful in almost any environment because their employers will be understanding and compassionate and their leadership successful.

Chapter 12

STYLE: A PART OF THE ADMINISTRATIVE FORMULA

Style is something everyone has an intuitive notion about but is often difficult to characterize. For a successful administrative career it is probably necessary that those in your employ understand your style as their group leader. How does an administrator decide about style? Does this start with self analysis or possibly psychoanalysis?

"Style...I don't know how to describe it, but I can respond to it!" "My style...I'm not sure, but I know I have one!" "Style...it changes with my job or it has to be changed!" "I can change it when I need to!" "I mostly have a hands-off style!" "My style is participatory!" I have a public style!" My leadership style is private!" "I am steady and persistent!" "You can describe my style in one word: tenacity!" "I am colorful or I am flamboyant!" "I am predictable!"

From this litany, the point is obvious: there are many different styles that are successful in different environments and may be evidenced by different leaders who are equally accomplished. The complexity of medicine allows great latitude of leadership style, but there may be some common characteristics that are more important to success than others.

Obviously, certain mandates may either preclude or mitigate against certain administrative styles. While certain positions may adopt the style of the knight of yesteryear and colorfully breeze through the halls of the institution expressing in dress and demeanor great individuality and independence, the CEO of others should best demonstrate dependability and responsibility. Deviation from this almost presribed behavior assumes an element of risk.

The medical institution needs from most administrators evidence of a great appreciation of the "bottom line," the inherent virtues of budgetary control, and favorable return on investment. Even if you technically perform these administrative tasks in a competent fashion, if you have a public, attention-getting, slightly unpredictable administrative style, whenever there is a mishap with use of resources you will be predictably asked to deal with the issue of your style. The investment in the resources that have been allocated to your area makes these expectations, by circumstance, legitimate for your parent institution. The successful CEO must appreciate the context in which he administrates. Physicians feel that they are the advocates for their patients. They would like to see their insistent style of demand reflected in the support or service administrator's compassionate style of response. Departments in medicine traditionally have reflected the character of the chief administrator, the chairman. Many departments were small in the number of personnel, and the CEO was often intimately involved in the service aspect of the departmental responsibility. The style of the CEO was observed by the members of the department as well as the clinicians, and everyone had a fairly comfortable (if not accurate) concept of what his style was. However, present day departments may consist of 50-plus rooms, $20 million to $30 million of equipment, and as many as 100 professionals practicing both subspecialty and supraspecialty medicine. At best, the department chairman may have only a superficial knowledge of the type of practice that occurs in any individual area of this vast complex and may possess no skill whatsoever in a performance subspecialty service, such as coronary balloon dilatation or interventive neuroradiology.

In this large semi-industrial complex, the administrators at the top will have difficulty projecting a personal style. In fact, it may be more realistic not to attempt to project a style, especially if it might differ from that which is expected by the department faculty, clinical colleagues, or the medical center administration. If the CEO of a service unit is perceived as predictable, workmanlike, dependable, and steady by those to whom he reports and supportive, understanding, and a facilitator to those over whom he must administrate, his "style" will be acceptable.

Some administrators would be perfectly comfortable and satisfied with this imposed "style." There are others who would find the external control unacceptable and who would insist upon more participation in the choice of style. The need for both creativity and independence is intrinsic in the self-concept of many administrators, and they feel compelled to express this in the style they project. Some want their personalities to be identified with a department that reflects the excitement of the resources at the administrator's command, the central and fundamental position of the administrator's department in the medical complex, and the change in the discipline from one of response to a specialty demonstrating an aggressive, proactive mode.

I believe style should be a part of the administrator's plan. While the externally created "style," or lack thereof, has a reasonable chance or preserving the administrator's position, it has almost no likelihood of advancing the discipline, fostering creativity, or nurturing a faculty or staff of independent scholars who feel "led." Adopting a style that advances one's department generates creativity, and encourages independence among the staff more than likely increasing the administrator's exposure and risk. However, the potential satisfaction from the department's accomplishments, the pleasure of participation in the creative process, and the excitement of aggressively pursuing the collective goal would seem to make obvious the correct choice of style.

Chapter 13

CHOOSING YOUR MENTORS

Administration is neither all intuitive nor totally learned, just as leadership is not entirely genetic or acquired. We have the complete range from self-help courses to seminars, or entire segments of graduate school training devoted to administrative leadership. However, one of the most important techniques leading to administrative success is choosing your mentors.

Mentors come in all sorts of configurations, both physical and emotional. Mentors can serve as role models that you can simply emulate, or they can assume the role of confidants. Probably the most determinative mentors are the facilitators, those who assist or cause something to occur which is favorable to your progress.There is even the negative role model: people for whom you toil who are sufficiently inept at administration that their style and techniques prove to be quite transparent, allowing you to avoid those circumstances that they recurrently find themselves in —ones which often lead to the detriment of their constituency.

As we mature as administrators, we become much more realistic in our consideration of mentors. In our youth, most often we would choose the absolute or "maximum leader" as a role model, individuals who possess knowledge of the absolute truth and a crystal clear mandate to guide their actions. This is certainly an inspirational figure, much on the order of George Patton, John Wayne, or Vince Lombardi. However, as we grow in our administrative relationships and perceive the complexity of a medical environment as opposed to war, movies, or the NFL, we recognize that acting in a manner which may have created the legend/myth of these individuals has limited practicality in the circumstance in which we must deliver.

In medical school, our mentors were usually personal heroes. The most popular one at my medical school was the founding dean who was legendary for his openness. Students, faculty, and all manner of people could walk into his office without an appointment or announced agenda and visit for any length of time: "the door was truly open." The dean would have his shirtsleeves rolled up and be engaged in nothing that he felt was as important as the message brought in by the visitor. Those junior faculty, who hoped to emulate this administrative style exactly, forgot several key points. The dean literally founded the medical school with his peers whom he brought with him; he possessed truly extraordinary communicative skills; he had enough energy to paddle his way out of the chaos that this approach to administration created; and life was simpler in the medical schools of the 30s, 40s, and 50s than it is today.

This legendary figure's immediate successor adopted a quite formal, even described as a "regal" style of administration, allowing the institution to regroup and to organize itself for a great period of expansion in the 70s and 80s under yet a third leader, who served as the modern mentor for a series of academic department chairmen, deans and vice chancellors (vice presidents) of several institutions. From this mentor, I, like others, learned the value of organizational planning and consensus building. Also, I learned the value of involvement of the lay community in any broad project of the medical institution.

During house staff training at some juncture, most ambitious, upwardly mobile residents will fantasize about becoming a departmental chairman. In casting about in this speculation, the most obvious role model and possible mentor is one's own leader. From my own observation, I believed that my chairman was successful because of faculty loyalty, and I attempted to discover how this had been engendered. He had trained a number of these people, but not the majority. They were widely separated in age, interests, and even national origin. There was no apparent divine game plan, and the department was so loosely organized that it appeared structureless. If any formal department meetings were ever held, the trainees were unaware of them. Yet the place ran, the morale seemed to be tolerable to good, and the acceptance by the faculty and institution was reasonable. To me, the reasons for this success were not readily apparent.

The chairman's greatest asset was honesty. He would sometimes be blunt but truthful. Trappings, honors, and posturing were almost treated with disdain. Since this was still in the era (pre-CT, MRI, etc.) of "plain film reading," his accomplishments in this area were legendary. It was recognized that his organizational skills, administrative instincts, and even his powers of communication were marginal, but they were tolerated and at times "coveted" by all, because with him you "knew where you stood." In fact, a great departmental and institutional pastime was reading the mood of the chairman. During my years as a resident and teaching fellow, I learned that if during any proposal or proffered plan of activity the chairman began massaging his eyebrows, you were not doing well. If, according to some, there was an obvious differential of skin appearance of his forehead (blanched on one side and erythematous on the other), the ball game was over and a timely exit was urgently appropriate. To impose this management style today would certainly invite disaster, but to select the endearing trait of forthrightness and unquestioned honesty as a subset of characteristics would certainly be advantageous to any administrator.

One might also reason that the choice of a mentor is often related to where you are in your own administrative career. If you are climbing the mountain, your mentor might appropriately be the goal-directed, disciplined workaholic whose single-mindedness will assure reaching the summit. If you are standing on the pinnacle (hopefully with both feet in contact with reality), you may need a planner/organizational leader as your mentor.

Many administrators find that it is much easier to create an empire than to manage one. One of the reasons for this difficulty is that they failed to change mentors and continued to use the same role models when their own expected roles and administrative environment had changed dramatically. Wyatt Earp never managed Tombstone after he cleaned it up, and Douglas MacArthur performed better in war than during peacetime. Most administrators can learn the custodial care and nurturing role of leadership of a mature institution if they will recognize the necessary change and choose different mentors. Note that even at the summit one needs mentors.

As a postdoctoral fellow, I had the good fortune to adopt a mentor who was my academic advisor, providing me access to someone who managed both a clinical and an academic department. His style, I later came to realize, was best described as "laissez faire." Although his physical presence in the clinical department was rare and his office was in the research area, there were few "hands on" visitations or departmental meetings, and no administrative memos for the direction of the individual members of this conglomerate, things seemed to get done. This management style was somewhere between cultivated detachment and benign neglect. The clinical staff had little or no contact with the basic scientists, yet each seemed to have a great deal of loyalty to the chairman and to the institution. In fact, the binding force seemed to be pride in the institution, and if a true mentor existed it was the image of that institution, an intangible concept which was very difficult to capture or even to understand. However, this lack of personal involvement by the mentor allowed this positive force to come to fruition.

While in this institution, I had administrative responsibilities for the research laboratories, grant funding, and fellows and graduate students. From time to time, it became necessary to visit my mentor, who by now had assumed responsibility for administration of the medical school, for advice and counsel. Presented with a specific administrative problem, he would answer with a response best described as a parable, so I always compared these encounters to a visit with Alice to Wonderland to see the Wizard of Oz. Only years later did I realize that these general utterances had wide and lasting applicability. They have been very helpful in administering a large, complex, and multi-dimensional enterprise.

In choosing your mentors, you may also determine (within certain limits) the type of mentor you will be. Early in my career, I had the opportunity to take an administrative position. At the time, I was only several years past residency training and had completed only my postdoctoral course work. My mentor never advised me not to succumb to the temptations and the trappings attendant to a departmental chairmanship. Instead, he asked me if I wanted to have a scholarly enterprise that would make significant academic contributions to our discipline. Understandably, I did. He then pointed out that to attract and maintain faculty and staff to engage in this undertaking, it would be necessary for them to see you as both experienced and accomplished in this endeavor. Thus, you must have the credentials to be this kind of role model or mentor. Without making me feel immature and naive, he had gently reminded me that he was my role model and that I had simply not established my reputation as a significant leader. I was also reminded that he had great credibility due to his tenure as an academician and also because he had been responsible for at least two major contributions to our discipline before taking an administrative position. Rather than leap for what I divined to be the equivalent of the brass ring or the coat of ermine, I spent the next few years in the research laboratories and observed my mentor as the medical school dean to prepare myself for future mentorship.

The adage that success breeds success can be thought about in people terms. Certainly, acting as an effective mentor makes it very likely that you will not only be successful in managing your own enterprise but that you will serve as a role model for future mentors among your constituency. Choosing your own mentors wisely and adapting the lessons from your observations of their ministry as a role model will be a very important factor in the success of your own administration.

Chapter 14

AN OFTEN NEGLECTED ADMINISTRATIVE RESPONSIBILITY: MENTORSHIP

Administration is often characterized in methodologies and in active discharge of one's perceived responsibilities. Certainly, administrators are much more successful in articulating and judging their influence upon employees in terms of action and response than in the creation of a general environment or in conducting their own affairs to serve as a role model. Facilitators are often identified for the tangible benefits that they provide for their employees. "Opening doors" and creating opportunities are usually accepted as responsibilities by almost all good administrators as part of the context in which they manage. For many employees, this will provide sufficient administrative leadership to make the institution efficient and successful. I would like from the provider side to consider the ill-defined but important concept of mentorship.

If one quantitates leadership, the activity of being a proper mentor might be judged so far down in the scale that it might not be viewed as an administrative technique at all. However, if one were to search for a common ingredient among successful medical administrators to identify the truly great ones, mentorship among the leaders would be the most common characteristic identified. Mentors and role models are what seems to activate the staff members to achieve their potential. Granted, the self starters will achieve a great deal simply by being placed in an environment that provides them adequate resources, but even these employees will further benefit by an appropriate role model. The majority of employees (talented individuals but not self actuated) can be both led and even inspired by the appropriate attitude and personal action by the administrative leaders.

In a service discipline, the staff must interact with colleagues as well as their patients. The quality of these interactions is often determined more by style than substance. The CEO has only a minor role in influencing the factual exchange that occurs between members of the staff but is quite determinant in the quality of this interaction. A posture of genuine concern for the welfare of their patients and compassion for their role as primary physician will almost ensure that the consultation be viewed as an appropriately helpful one. Administrators should recognize that their personal style will be viewed as the benchmark by their own employees and by the referring physicians as well. While this fact may obtain in the referring specialties, it is especially important in service ones.

For years, in a quite well-known institution, the chief of a surgical subspecialty had a national reputation for his clinical acumen as well as his gentlemanly style in the consultative process. His faculty recognized this to be the accepted methodology for their interaction with patients and other disciplines. Their practice was quite successful, and they were viewed by their colleagues in the institution as a department that was pleasant to work with and were responded to in kind. With retirement of the chief of the service, a new administrative director was brought from a citadel of excellence who came highly acclaimed for his academic accomplishments. Soon it became apparent that his professional style was one in which no amount of service would avoid criticism, characterized by a failure to adopt an institutional posture and conform to the professional ethic of the service departments accepted as appropriate by other referring services.

An increasingly demanding attitude, if not responded to, would predictably result in an unpleasant confrontation. Initially, this new leader was given extraordinary service in an effort to gain time to have him understand and accept the routine practices of other disciplines in the institution. Unfortunately, he and, more importantly, his staff interpreted the turn of events as affirmation of their method to more effectively gain use and control of institutional resources. The chief of service became the role model for behavior in his department. Soon, fellow physicians and those in the consultative services attempted to limit their interaction with the group as much as possible. Additionally, referring physicians in the area and community changed their patterns of referral, and the patients for that surgical subspecialty dwindled to an unacceptable few. Whether the chief of service ever realized that the role model he represented became the "mentorship" for his service is unclear. Rather than accept the responsibility, he had his service engage in heroic measures to attract referrals. However, these efforts were largely unsuccessful, because they were not accompanied by any noticeable attitudinal changes.

A more appropriate response would have been for the chief of service to have responded to the widespread criticism of his service, change his attitude and demeanor, and observe whether or not his faculty did likewise. Behavior modification for adults is difficult, but to establish the appropriate role model in a medical unit, leaders must accept the responsibility to change if they are not providing the type of image necessary for their staff to emulate.

Mentorship requires more than creating the physical or even fiscal environment, as I have previously noted. To act as a mentor, one must be visibly involved. In the clinical areas, participation in conducting rounds or the actual treatment of cases are all options that the administrative officer has. For institutional administrators, attendance and participation in appropriate committees and conferences to demonstrate interest and involvement are necessary. These roles, if fulfilled with an attitude of enthusiasm, represent opportunities to serve as a visible role model and can be perceived as a forum for the CEO to create standards of appropriate behavior.

Observing medical institutions over the past three decades, it became clear to me that those groups which had an appropriate standard bearer - an administrative leader who demonstrated the proper ongoing mentorship - have been the most successful. Granted, institutional support and other external factors were important, but the major determinant seems to be the quality of mentorship exercised by the CEO.

Most analysts and administrative "soothsayers" explain managerial success in terms of style and technique; mentorship is about substance. This is not a programmatic response, nor is it a plan that can be adopted by every administrator as a blueprint to success. Mentorship, while leading to some universal goals such as satisfying collegial relationships, the image of responsibleness, an attitude of compassion and concern, institutional pride, active and enthusiastic pursuit of common goals, and productivity, must be a conscious effort by the CEO to adopt the potentially successful role model specific to that institution.

For most administrative leaders, the creation of a role model to achieve proper mentorship is not an active consideration, but it should be. This is an administrative responsibility not generally recognized as existent by most CEOs, yet it can set the posture and define the image of the institution in a fundamental manner. The importance of understanding this role and acceptance of the responsibility by the chief administrative officer may be critical to the overall success of the institutional effort.

Chapter 15

MICROMANAGEMENT WILL YIELD MICROACCOMPLISHMENTS

Somewhere there must be an administrative strategy that does not overdose on the technical aspects of management and gives proper emphasis to the care and feeding of people. However, to be a recognized soothsayer in the field of administration, conventional wisdom is that you must eloquently espouse the virtue of the technical correctness of some form of management. This may be applicable in the widget industry or the manufacture of cookie cutters, but it often falls short in complex industries providing services to human beings.

I always marvel at the physician who wishes to become an "administrator" and sails forth to a fast and untidy course at some management school. They usually emerge with a new vocabulary and a series of standard plans to make the operation more efficient and effective. In context, these new acquisitions of management techniques will be helpful, but should they obscure logic, ethics and courtesy, their virtues may not be realized. The other little affectation I have noticed is that charts and diagrams can replace consensus and understanding and that memoranda and directives will be generated by the hour — or minute. Policy will become so rigid that it will be perceived, by the flock, as a constraint to their progress. Managing is no longer a means to an end but becomes the end itself.

One might expect that this administrative change would meet with resistance, but it interestingly results in the negative form, competition, and staff often become "score keepers" and spend most of their time and energy determining whether the other employees are accepting their fair share of the constraints these directives have imposed. Everyone seems to get caught up in this micromangement because it represents the most personal form of control that exists.

Most normal humans tend to avoid control, but to creative people it is an anathema. Micromanagement is the most effective antidote to originality that I know of. Creative staff may momentarily embrace an environment because it initially appears safe, predictable, and ever compassionate because it projects a protective image. Once the control element of micromanagement becomes apparent to creative persons, they will marshal their considerable skills and energies to escape this vise. A corollary to this response is that the unimaginative, passive staff will find the environment of micromangement to be safe and warm; over a period of time, the character of the staff will change to favor this group.

A great deal of human behavior is an attempt to gain control or in a response to an external control. I believe that creativity can be directed, but it cannot be controlled. Micromanagers like to portray themselves as enablers, but, in truth, they facilitate to gain control. Their "help" is a method of achieving an obligation, and their involvement (however well intended in its external appearance) will soon acquire the characteristics of monitoring. In fact, micromangers have a fatal tendency to attempt to control the data or other results of the effort, even though they are usually unaware of it.

One of the telling clues that you have come under the spell of a micromanager is when they repeatedly use the term "mission" to describe what they believe to be a common goal. My experience with "missions" dates back to the 1960s in Southeast Asia; thus, I have always believed that this was to emphasize the gravity the micromanager wanted to convey regarding their personal wishes to the multitude. If one accepts it as a "mission" then it becomes *the* plan, not *a* plan; and since it is the micromanager's plan, one does not have to be a Fulbright scholar to divine who is in charge. Back to control again.

Micromanagers had rather generate diagrams and flow charts than almost anything. Remember Reggie Jackson's analogy about the home run? If you don't, you may have the makings of a micromanager. An outgrowth of this compulsion is to create titles so that one can fill in the boxes or have the flow charts complete so that everyone has an "identity" however contrived. Usually, the lines of management are so overlapped that they become obscured, and turf is perceived as doled out and apportioned by memo and not by accommodations worked out by reasonable people. In fact, trust among staff can be greatly eroded by memos, flow charts and titles, while the manager may feel comfortable and *really* in control. Control of what? Possibly chaos from the rank and file.

Someday, watch a great wide receiver on a broken play. The genius is not in the fact that he executed the pattern but in the creativity he exercised after the initial plan went awry. The Pro Bowl quarterback did not get there because he personally directed the blocking assignments of every member of his offensive line. He annunciated the objective and may have globally judged the results, but those lineman assumed the specific responsibility of their role.

Micromangement is said to be derived from insecurity. Understanding its origin does not seem to make it more acceptable. One of the reasons is that it conveys an arrogance that goes like "my way or the highway" or "if I want it done correctly, I should see to it myself." This doesn't leave any space, and humans, especially the type that seek careers in the health service field, like space. Micromangement also thwarts the achievement reward of others because they never feel what they did was entirely their idea but may have been the micromanager's. Humans enjoy good ideas, but they are ecstatic about ***their*** great ideas. Micromanagers convey the idea that only they have the good ones. So the flock can only have a "good" idea if they convince the micromanager that they either got the idea from them or they were inspired by a related idea from the same origin. The effort required for this type of posturing is both tiring and boring. It always reminds me of the involved movement of the mating ritual of certain exotic fowl: by the time all the strutting is done, each may have forgotten what it was all about. The appellation "bird brained" may have a profound meaning in micromanagement strategy.

The lack of confidence of the micromanager is manifested by the compelling need to control and this infects the staff with an insecurity that makes them hesitant to perform. In fact, they may expend considerable energy in non-doing or only acting within what they believe the confines of their title to be. Heaven forbid that it be "Master of the Hounds", "Chancellor of the Exchequer" or "Comptroller". I never have determined what a comptroller is, but the similarity to controller concerns me greatly.

Are there any virtues to micromangement? For a while, the micromanager feels in control, and maybe the super-manager feels informed because he has all the memos, flow charts and diagrams so that he can fill the great filing cabinet in the sky. If the talented and creative leave quietly, then it may simply be forever before they are missed, or they may not be missed at all because it is difficult to miss what they *would* have achieved. You do not miss the forty foot jumper you never saw.

Is there a place for micromanagers in a complex environment such as a medical institution? Someone should be in charge of parking validation, lost x-ray films, and stolen medical records; maybe the "gofer" on the team to prepare for the JCAH. Actually, there is a time in which I would aspire to be a micromanager—when responding to the IRS' request for more documentation.

Micromanagement leads to microthinking and eventually to microachievement. However, these achievements will be well documented, and those achievers who are left will know exactly where they fit in the diagram and exactly who is in charge.

Chapter 16

DELEGATION IN A MEDICAL INSTITUTION

As administrators, we are caught in a massive web of responsibilities that extends to every part of our lives. There is usually so much to be done that responsibilities must be shared among the staff. The division of responsibility and the quality of the cooperative effort determine how well the goals of the institution will be accomplished. Many personal and organizational issues easily become entangled in this sharing of assignments. Delegation is the primary link between the needs of the medical complex and the functioning of the individual staff.

Becoming an effective delegator requires self-examination for issues that may involve personal security, leadership qualities, motivational style, and relationship to the institution being served. When barriers to effective delegation are addressed and resolved, the self-confidence of each individual in the administrative structure increases and the assignments are completed more efficiently. Patterns of delegation reveal a wealth of information as to how a medical institution functions both formally and informally. The administrator's involvement with organizations often extends far beyond the office. Understanding the structural principles of delegation will facilitate a greater awareness of the institutional psychology and how it may affect the productivity of the administrator, the group, and the institution.

Each institution has a set of values by which it functions and self actuates. The values may not be clearly articulated, but they powerfully shape the behavior of the staff who work within that particular system. These values also determine the division of responsibility in the individual units and how tasks are performed. In addition, these values determine the general atmosphere in that institutional environment at every level. Examples of the values that determine delegation patterns are centralized control (versus sectional autonomy), trust in individuals (versus myriad "checking" devices), and responsiveness to individuals and their needs (as opposed to getting the work done regardless of its impact on the staff). Delegation patterns define the real lines of authority. Despite the fact that every department and institution has a formal structure that can easily be diagrammed, there is also an informal structure that may diverge in significant ways from the organization chart. The important concept is "Who does what work under whose authority?" The next question is "How closely does this network of responsibility and authority reflect the formal structure of the department?" When there is disparity in a department between formal administrative structure and informal delegation networks, the informal structure is usually viewed as more significant; thus, the structure of delegation is effectively the structure of the institution. It is logical but naive to view delegation only in terms of organizational productivity. The adequacy of delegation can either impede or facilitate the growth of those staff who perform the tasks emanating from professional responsibilities.Delegation defines not only the lines of authority but also the emotional atmosphere of the administrative office as it influences the development of individuals. That critical ambiance can either enhance the medical unit or detract from its effectiveness, depending on how well the patterns of delegation meet the basic needs of the perception of the individual staff.

Delegation not only defines the lines of authority but also has tremendous psychological impact on everyone who works within that environment. Beyond the structural principles of delegation, the psychology of delegation must also be understood by the administrator. In this structure of delegation is enough psychological power to significantly influence positively or negatively the productivity of an institution. The basic functions of delegation have a significant "people component."

Quality leadership and skill in effective delegation are internally related. In simple terms, leaders of excellence delegate well. Ineffective leaders who are not respected by their subordinates usually have problems delegating authority in positive ways. Closely examining the patterns of delegation is one means to determine effective and weak leaders in an institution like a health care facility. There are usually some of both types in every institution, and staff members invariably know who they are.

A great deal of administrative inefficiency in medical institutions has its origin in delegation problems. The difficulties may lie with specific individuals or be the result of a maladaptive delegation style widespread within an entire unit. The adequacy of delegation determines not only the quality and quantity of medicine that is delivered but also whether tasks are completed on time if completed at all. Closely examining and restructuring the delegation of responsibility is an important step to enhancing efficiency.

Assigned responsibilities should create personal challenge and individual growth. However, over-delegation to a few individuals compromises the "challenge factor" and substitutes stress and pressure for reward. At the other extreme, having too little to do or no challenge in the administrative unit quickly diminishes motivation and creates lethargy. In either circumstance, individual stress and distress will be to the detriment of those who do the work, not to mention the negative impact on the institution itself. For an institution to grow, responsibility for many of its tasks must be shifted from the staff to subordinates. These individuals must be trusted to accomplish these delegated tasks efficiently. When a few senior staff retain most of the responsibility and authority, they cannot "let go" to delegate, the institution cannot effectively expand.

In all areas of life, those individuals who are not challenged do not mature in capability and judgment. The relationship of this fact to delegation is obvious: an institution can develop its leadership through effective delegation, or it can just as easily inhibit the growth of the potential leaders. Creating new leaders from within by delegating responsibility and supporting reasonable autonomy is the characteristic of a healthy medical institution.

Under-delegation or abusive delegation causes momentum and morale to decline. Morale is that essential feeling in the staff members that they are valued, that their work is appreciated, and that they are an important part of the institutional mission. Appropriate delegation does much to enhance this important motivational factor. Proper delegation also generates loyalty; because "people needs" are being met and the individual staff cares about the overall responsibility.

Many medical responsibilities are quite complex and require a cooperative effort for completion. Delegation can foster a strong cooperative effort and commitment to accomplish the task in a timely fashion. Conversely, ineffective delegation can generate the perception of lack of caring or even subtle sabotage of the tasks that need to be accomplished to render the expected service.

Many projects are delayed or scuttled entirely because of problems in delegation. The issues that cause such difficulties may be either individual or organizational. There are many personal styles of delegation, and there are just as many psychological issues that become mired in the assignment of responsibility. There are several problem-producing roles that administrators fall into: dumping delegators, who shift far too much responsibility to others without assuming a legitimate part of the responsibility themselves; and the solo artists, who delegate too little work or authority. Such individuals are found in almost every department of any size.

Lateral delegation involves persuading a colleague, usually at a similar level in the medical organization, to assume the responsibility for one's own work. This maneuver will allow shifting of responsibilities to others of equal accomplishment. Passive or compliant colleagues can become primary victims. The most effective way to curtail abusive lateral shifting is to encourage potential victims to say "no;" but this may require working out their personal vulnerabilities or fears associated with that response. The effort required to discourage lateral shifting will result in enhanced morale among staff members, and management will benefit because it will be perceived as caring.

Shifting "up line" delegation is a method whereby legitimate responsibility for decision-making is passed upward. This takes time, and while waiting for a response, responsibilities that could be discharged are not even initiated. The effect of this kind of denial of responsibility is organizational inefficiency, as everything takes much more time than needed. The most effective way to discourage the up-line shift is to turn responsibility back to the level in the organization where specific decisions should be made. The administration can ease this correction by trusting and supporting the judgments made at lower levels. Up-line shifting can be indirectly promoted by a facility that sometimes punishes subordinates for making legitimate decisions. Acquiring staff who are secure in their leadership capabilities is the most effective solution.

A procrastination habit means that tasks are avoided until the last minute and then often shifted to the staff to complete under the extreme pressure of an impending deadline. In many instances, staff members are made to work overtime, evenings, or weekends to overcome the problems caused by a procrastinating leader who has not been attentive to current responsibilities. Staff resentment and lack of respect for such managers flourishes, but subordinates usually lack the authority to prevent this abusive pattern. When procrastination results from miscommunication about what must be done and when, it must be dealt with organizationally. The roots, however, may lie in a disorganized administrator who cannot set priorities or properly anticipate deadlines. Often, time-management training in combination with some very clear expectations from "upstairs" may be helpful.

To some administrators, leadership means giving all possible work to subordinates so that personal interests can be pursued. These interests may include unrelated meetings or failing to be present when needed to actively participate in the responsibilities of their constituency. Staff members feel they are being abused, and their leader has abdicated the personal responsibility necessary for them to work together efficiently. Management training will not provide the motivation to create necessary involvement in the affairs of the institution. Such a manager may be experiencing burnout, and that must be addressed. Upper management must identify such individuals and design specific interventions to help them renew their motivation.

Another type of administrator could be characterized as the previously noted "solo artist." For certain emotional reasons, solo artists want to manage it all. The result is that they cannot or will not delegate responsibility that should be entrusted to others. Inability to delegate creates self-imposed pressure and stress on the administrator and has a negative impact on staff members. The perfectionist is one example of a solo artist. It has been said that "perfectionists are people who take great pains and then give them to others!" They also tend to be incapable delegators. Perfectionists often distrust the work of their staff because it rarely meets their concept of high standards. They would rather complete a task themselves and have it done "right" according to personal expectations in lieu of accepting the efforts of their employees, although the staff performance may well meet the needs of the institution. In the meantime, the constantly critical attitude of the perfectionist will lower the self-esteem of staff members who are entirely capable of performing adequate work.

The perfectionist administrator should not let excessively high personal standards obstruct the tasks that must be done or the service to be rendered. Learning by this administrator to respond to the positive attributes of others would also be helpful. When these two skills are learned, efficiency improves, morale increases, and the perfectionist does not get so burned out. If these skills cannot be learned by the administrator, ultimately the medical unit must decide if the "quality" performance of the perfectionist is worth the morale problems being created among the rest of the staff.

An insecure administrator is easily and often threatened by the competence of others, including subordinates. The manager characterized as the defensive denier is especially fearful of bright, motivated, and aggressive junior staff. Even competent staff members can be perceived to be threats to a person in a position of power that does feel secure in this role. As a result, the administrator does not delegate important work to these young, aggressive staff, or subordinates are denied key tasks that would help them learn essential management skills. Further, skilled staff members are often unduly criticized and given too little credit for their accomplishments.

The defensive denier's administrative style is to keep others subordinate as a method of coping with the denier's high levels of personal insecurity. There are many causes for this maladaptive leadership style. At times, insecurity in a managerial role causes this problem, and training in specific leadership skills may assist. At other times, such an individual has risen to a level of personal incompetence—the Peter Principle—and additional technical training or a lateral shift in responsibility may be necessary. There are also occasions when the institution is to blame for giving no job security to administrators, and all become defensive. In such instances, a shift in policy may be necessary.

The overcontrolling administrator will state, "We run a tight ship here." No one is permitted autonomy in this institution. All control, even down to the most minute detail, must remain in the administrator's hands. Great energy is expended needlessly in monitoring others to make sure that the task is performed "just right." Because there is little trust, there is little delegation, and this administrator may be perceived to work against staff members instead of with them. Like the defensive denier, the overseer punishes competence. Over-control of mundane aspects of work must be relaxed and autonomy granted for the brightest and the best to remain. Working directly with staff members in a mentor relationship is helpful. In addition, pairing this kind of individual with a very flexible supervisor often will obviate an unfavorable outcome.

"Head of the family" administrators are very people-oriented individuals who want to keep a hand in everything and run a growing unit as a close-knit family. Inevitably, working hours become longer to maintain the personal contact with all staff members and to remain personally involved in all aspects of the operation. New and needed management systems may not be implemented, and key personnel are not hired. The patriarch or matriarch administrator eventually suffers, as does the work of the institution.

For an institution to grow, delegation must occur. Management systems that are sensitive to the needs of the individual staff and the work environment must be implemented, and the administrator can always maintain close contact with staff members through regular visits to the office. In the interim, competent and people-oriented staff are given responsibility for the day-to-day functioning of various services.

Delegation is good management, and management is delegation. In the past, many corporate definitions of management focused exclusively on the bottom line of the ledger sheet. This limited orientation can exclude sensitivity to people who did the work or to the psychological needs of the staff. Such tunnel vision is now being seen as a major flaw in management theory. A strategy for enhancing productivity includes strong emphasis on the quality of the work environment, a sensitivity to the needs of employees for personal fulfillment and satisfaction, and attention given to enhancing morale in the institution. Delegation, effective or problematic, in large part determines all these important corporate qualities and is germane to the issues in all areas.

Beyond effective delegation, there are several additional techniques that the administrative leadership can take to enhance the outcome after reaching an equitable division of responsibility. Although sometimes personally difficult to put into practice, these guidelines will help to make the administrator a mature and trusted leader. CEOs must stand by the work they have delegated to others. If administrators constantly reverse decisions or undo their own delegation or that of others, the incentive to do quality work in the unit will deteriorate, and the relationship with staff will be compromised.

Constantly and consistently reinforce the positive in your staff. Describe your staff with pride both publicly and privately. As a good administrator, share the credit generously. Also, delegate the task - not how it is to be performed. This philosophy permits staff members to work in ways comfortable to them or to innovate. Creative talent is unleashed, and the delegator gets the work done as well.

Power issues, independence and dependence, perception of masculine and feminine roles, and adequacy of communication all play a part in delegation. Confronting and resolving these kinds of psychological issues help to train managers to be leaders in their fields. No manager can ever forget that personal leadership style is a powerful determinant of staff morale, motivation, and productivity.

Chapter 17

CULTIVATED DETACHMENT: AN EFFECTIVE ADMINISTRATIVE TECHNIQUE

Often, the emphasis in communications regarding various administrative styles and ploys is upon those techniques effective in building departments or programs. There is a dearth of publications dealing with the subject of management of institutions and medical programs that are functioning and mature. This communication will deal with a technique many have found quite effective that I think of as "cultivated detachment or benign neglect."

When institutions are in the formative stages, emphasis is placed upon acquisition of resources. Division heads uniformly have such great space, technical, and people needs that the focus of interest is a global one. Many times the task seems to require such an outlay of energy that little effort is spent in the assessment of equity and fairness. Enthusiasm for the general effort is at such a high level that everyone seems to be in accord. The institutional administrators have often made sufficient philosophical, legal and moral commitments to the effort that most activities appear to be an expression of "exercising the mandate" and the avant garde programs an extension of the same. Everything seems possible and this attitude is often shared by the individual services who want "great" departments so that they can institute new programs and offer new capabilities based upon the success and acquisitions of any of the particular segments.

Into this benevolent and compassionate environment one can impose innovative programs and research facilities. The unit can expect to be granted common space resources by the institution, accept collaborative overtures from other areas, and even to receive gifts by some of the "major" disciplines. Because there is so much to accomplish initially and the goals appear so clearly defined, each unit has the impression that they are independently progressing toward a goal that will contribute to the common good. The spirit of cooperation in this type of environment abounds; collecting, acquiring and instituting are generally creative and as long as this mode can be sustained, general goodwill will usually be maintained.

However, the above described overall growth will subsequently evolve into either stability of the unit with selected areas of short term expansion or a stable environment with emphasis upon management of those resources already acquired. For the remainder of the twentieth century the scenario for medicine may well be that of consolidation and even retrenchment. A common phenomenon in all of these circumstances is realization by all involved in the process that resources are finite and that their opportunities for growth and future advancement may have limits. Implicit in this realization also is that distribution of these resources may be on a competitive basis, and within a particular unit the allocations may be uneven and there may come to exist "haves" and "have-nots." Concerns of equity and fairness often arise among staff within the institutions at the time of this revelation of finite resources. Intradepartmental issues of "turf" and equivalent contribution ("Is a fifteen-minute physical exam equal to five chest radiographs, or two ECG studies?") will often become important.

In view of cost containment initiatives such as DRGs, RAPS and RVS, the bargaining threat of HMOs and PPOs and the escalating challenge of medical malpractice litigation, institutional administrators may feel that fixed expenditures for space and capital equipment represent a financial risk which they do not wish to incur. Even approved capital investments are entered into quite reluctantly with what seems to be an extraordinary series of checks and balances. Responsibility shifts often cause interminable delays in purchase orders and multiple sets of cost analyses, income projections and "break even" calculations that are required in much greater numbers. Certain areas may no longer be universally viewed as a given revenue source, and the capital and personal expenditures have such a high unit cost that they can be recognized by those formulating institutional policy as investment risks with extremely high visibility.

As medical institutions become mature, staff mobility will decrease. Those aggressive, young staff will have better identified their own needs and the activities in which they wish to participate. In the process, they also will have acquired a group of professional dependents and a set of resources in their units for which they must fill the role as chief advocate. Some of your staff will be very comfortable in this activity while others will not — but all will benefit by increasing their experience. Since by this time the internal resources of the institution will not accommodate the perceived needs of the staff, compromise will have become an ongoing process. If this compromise is imposed "from above" by the CEO, significant questions of equity and fairness will invariably arise.

If under guidance and counsel of the administrator the competing staff are allowed to seek their own accommodation, then they are more likely to feel responsible for and responsive to the final decision. At times the process may be painfully deliberate for the administrative leader, but acceptance of the decision or later redefinition of the outcome by their constituency makes the initial investment of time and exercise of patience worthwhile.

When a faculty member or group has a proposal requiring institutional resources, in most medical institutions the tendency is to hand the gauntlet to the CEO and have them sally forth, or give the manager a brief and let him appear on "the day in court" with the deliberative body. At best, the staff will often view whatever the decision as one reached by a compromise between the administrator and the institution or that the verdict of the administration was thrust upon the leader. The later circumstance becomes an invitation to engage in the honored Greek tradition of "kill the messenger."

Using the administrative technique of cultivated detachment or benign neglect, the CEO can choose not to be the "champion of the colors" but have the staff not only prepare their own case, but plead it as well. At first the administration may wish to deal only with the administrator of the unit and the staff may be uncomfortable with the lead role (it is sort of lonely at the "point") but if the CEO insists upon this mode of interaction it may eventually gain acceptance by all.

Intradepartmental turf issues in medicine are somewhat more problematic than those from without because no common "enemy" or competitor can be agreed upon. Concerns of fairness and equity among one's staff result in many requests to have the CEO act as the judge, jury, and apportioner of resources. Often if the chairperson chooses not to decide upon competing requests of considerable merit, the staff will work out a compromise themselves, each recognizing the virtues and limitations of the other's proposal and being satisfied with the decision they have reached jointly. Staff will often request that the administration develop a complicated formula for compensation, research opportunities, travel and vacation based upon a clearly understood and universally accepted criteria. If the chair will not succumb to the temptation of this request, with time the faculty will provide great insight as to the criteria they agree upon, something not likely to occur they believe these were not "their" decisions. Quantification of service or the value of a task by a third party (such as the CEO) has little chance of being perceived as just or accurate.

Often, accommodations between disciplines can be formulated only by the staff involved, and not by the administrators. In the governance of medical resources, the advise and consent process is effective if the players themselves perform the process and not the appointed nonparticipant judges. The chairman (CEO) must engage in benign neglect if this process is to occur. This administrator will often be encouraged to do otherwise by other administrators that have neither the wisdom nor maturity to engage in this technique. These medical managers must negotiate with their "equals" if this means equally uninformed.

Creative people often feel as encumbered by imposed "facilitation" on the part of the leader as they do by perceived barriers to their progress that the CEO may erect. If the staff does not have sufficient opportunity to exercise their originality, they often have an incomplete feeling of their progress or control of their destiny, even if successful. A great deal of creativity and originality can be productively expended in solving those problems of greatest interest to them if they perceive that they have a minimum of external control. Staff "cultivate" with these successes in their own eyes, although many administrative leaders do not sufficiently appreciate the fact that they do.

Highly motivated people often have difficulty sharing the benefits of success and are not very tolerant of a leader who receives benefit by virtue of their visible position. This then becomes an issue of the administrators contribution. Cultivated detachment or benign neglect will minimize the opportunity for this circumstance to arise. The staff will more clearly see the environment in which the administrator functions and will appreciate the advise and consent process. Credit for service performed is a major issue and a leader must be attuned to their staff's perception of fairness in this regard.

Thus far my discussion has emphasized the benefits of "cultivated detachment or benign neglect" in relation to the institution. The greatest benefit of this technique may be to the CEO or chairpersons themselves. One of the most difficult realizations that an administrator must come to is that many of the perceived problems cannot be solved and some challenges cannot be overcome personally by them. The administration does not have to be the universal "white knight" for the departmental staff or the "perfect child" for the institutional administration. After practicing this described administrative technique for even a short time, the unrelenting pressure to assume those roles lessens and the feeling of freedom often stimulates creativity in the administrator. I believe that a chair or CEO should continue to engage in research, write and have a personal area in which to make original contributions—practicing this technique will be helpful in providing the time and emotional energy to make this possible. Also, the greatness of an institution is certainly a reflection of the sum or hopefully the multiple of its component parts. By this method, the total should be much larger.

Chapter 18

VOIR DIRE: A TRADITIONAL LEGAL TECHNIQUE THAT CAN LEAD TO ADMINISTRATIVE SUCCESS

Achieving a consensus is the administrative goal which eventually leads to long-term and continued success. A major determinant in this process is to acquire a constituency. Most administrators, at some level, recognize that this must be the purpose but fail to employ a simple and effective management technique that will significantly increase their chances of success — the management equivalent to the legal ploy of jury selection of *voir dire*. In seeking a consensus, one has the same purpose as in the selection of a jury: to seek the truth through espousal of a particular line of reasoning.

In the legal profession, the "truth" is the primacy of a particular line of reasoning which is accepted above the other alternative(s) by the trier of fact, the jury. In other words, the legal truth is not an absolute but is that which is decided by a body before which one has presented his respective data. What is deemed correct is that which is selected by the judging group from the presentation of a body of fact. The acceptance of fact is largely dependent upon the bias that was brought to the deliberative forum by the trier. This inherent tendency to choose a particular line of reasoning may be unrecognized by the juror but will be fully appreciated by the successful attorney during the litigation process. It should also be recognized in selection of participants to seek a consensus and constituency by the successful medical administrator.

Voir dire is, in essence, a procedure whereby a body of individuals is selected to hear a specific pleading. Theoretically, the litigants, acting through advice of counsel, are better ensured a fair hearing and trial through this process. This procedure is designed to eliminate those jurors who, by virtue of their personal beliefs for whatever cause, would be biased. This does not imply that any negative motives be accorded the potential jurors but speaks only to their somewhat prejudicial reception of the evidence and interpretation thereof. As a poignant example, a juror not believing in the deterrent value of the death penalty should not serve in a first-degree murder trial.

Attorneys are at a disadvantage when compared to medical administrators because attorneys are supplied with a limited personal profile and have a narrow time period to question the potential jurors to discover their bias and prejudices. The medical CEO, on the other hand, has greater knowledge of these characteristics manifest by other physicians on staff and the administrators of their particular institution. Given the usual abilities of judging human conduct, the CEO will have a reasonable idea of the prejudices and biases of these staff individuals. The *voir dire* option will be only partially available to the administrator; however, inasmuch as it can be utilized, it should be employed to the fullest extent permitted. Hopefully, some examples of the effective use of this technique may be instructive.

In the past decade, exclusive contracts to provide certain medical services were negotiated between the CEO of that unit and the institutional administration, but more recently, competing disciplines have requested and often been granted significant representation in these deliberations. In the future, one might imagine that the full hospital medical board or the executive professional staff of the institution will insist upon genuine involvement.

Historically, hospital administrators wanted to have these exclusive contracts because they ensured the presence of certain services deemed essential to the medical and financial viability of the hospital. Thus, it was thought to be to the advantage of the CEO to meet and negotiate the exclusive contract with the hospital administration alone. The administrator will attempt to persuade the hospital that meeting together without other physician or professional staff involvement might be to mutual advantage. However, this isolation tended both to estrange the advocates and decision makers from other physicians and to separate the rewarding of exclusive contracts and the granting of professional staff privileges.

These acquired responsibilities provide the accepting physicians sufficient professional exposure and liability that they should insist upon the active involvement of other physicians, obviously preferring those disciplines that should not be inherently biased due to their competition for "turf" with those staff physicians seeking an exclusive contract. *Voir dire*, in both selecting the participants and setting the agenda, should be fully employed by the prudent CEO of the competing administrative unit.

Recent developments in the issue of exclusive contracts have somewhat clouded the considerations of the composition of the jury for exclusive contract negotiations. Hospitals and medical management companies have realized that they can often contract for exclusive medical service contracts at lower cost than the traditional arrangements. They do not often address such issues as responsiveness, professional competence, or standards of care in these deliberations. Rather than ascribe the responsibilities to the province of the professional board, hospitals and their attorneys have insisted that these are purely financial decisions to address economic issues and are not subject to due process by affected referring or hospital-based physicians. In a *voir dire* procedure, prior to challenges, those requesting the exclusive contract must ensure the participation of their fellow physician colleagues.

Decisions regarding the acquisition of sophisticated and expensive resources traditionally have been almost entirely deliberated between the providers and hospital administration. As the costs, complexities, and compensation for certain medical procedures have become increasingly unpredictable, other physicians and even members of institution boards of trust have requested greater participation. This should be encouraged by the CEO of the provider group if, along with his staff, they are willing to build a constituency among the referring physicians. This technique will, of necessity, be applied in terms of standard of care and patient welfare. By assuring the referring physician access to a new technology and by establishing oneself as the most qualified to employ and nurture this new service, the CEO may not only create a constituency but a very compelling advocate. They may even select as a potential member of the decision group a colleague who may also wish to use the equipment.

While there is an element of risk in this *voir dire* activity, CEOs will have a great opportunity to convince their colleagues that, by the group having all of a particular resource, this will move them toward mutual self-interest and to their patients also. At the very least, the CEO might show the potential competitors the demanding responsibilities of financing these resources while offering as an inducement the concept of an integrated service to ensure efficient patient care.

The most compelling reasons for involving one's own staff in any activities affecting the whole of the unit is to gain access to their advice and perspective. Committees should not only reflect the purpose of the group but the expertise of the members as well. A global and long-range issue should be addressed by a mix of staff who have been former members of the unit as well as others who are newer and more prone to independent, even nontraditional thinking. Never "load" any committee with those viewed as "senior citizens" but recognize that in any large group there are several constituencies, each of whom feel deserving of representation. An acute problem necessitating a "quick fix" may be more amenable to a *voir dire* selection of the more aggressive, provocative members of the medical unit. The CEO must remember that the insurance for an inappropriate *voir dire* decision in this circumstance falls in the Good Samaritan analysis and logic: one must simply have more latitude to be less than perfect.

To paraphrase Marshall MacLuhan, "the budget is the message." This principle should be recalled in the selection process of the members of the budget committee of a medical institution. Unquestionably, there are team players who will be mindful of the institutional or group constraints in this process, and then there are others who will overwhelmingly invoke the "free enterprise" model. Unless one is truly blessed with a Joe Montana, a Michael Jordan or a Roger Clemmons in his group, it is necessary to select a preponderance of team players to assist with the budgetary process. The franchise is generally more important than the player, and compensation and resource allocation inequities, if blatant, will significantly affect group performance.

It is also important to keep in mind that this is a quantifiable reward and can be gauged by the individual members of the *institution* in human terms — purchasing power. By *voir dire* selection, it is possible to elicit an understanding, informed, and erudite advocacy group for these budgetary decisions should they be challenged from without or, later, within.

Thus, administrative success for the CEO can be greatly enhanced by careful selection of the participants in any particular institutional activity. *Voir dire* is not only a technique available to the administration but one that should be employed in a considered manner. In the interactions with one's parent institution, the choice of participants may be limited but should be sought as an effective alternative to group deliberations in which someone other than the CE0 has chosen the participants and possibly dictated the agenda accordingly.

Chapter 19

COMPLEX MANDATES: DEPARTMENTAL CEOS

Historically, the CEO of a medical department is an aggressively sought position. The European model of "the Professor" placed the chairman in an exalted position in relation to the staff. This was the position to which many physicians aspired. While the advantages of the chair were well known, the criteria by which these administrators were evaluated were not well defined. Chairs often were faculty members who had progressed through the various levels of departmental appointment and were usually chosen for their clinical and research acumen. These, as noted, have left physicians untrained and ill-prepared for the challenges they face. Outside of medicine certain societal changes have created issues that are now to be addressed. As an example, prior to 1975, medicine had been immune to the regulations and analysis of antitrust legislation. The landmark cases of *Goldfarb v. Virginia State Bar* and the *Rex Hospital* case declared that if one of the "learned professions" acted in a business sense, then that profession would be held to the standards and regulations of the Sherman Antitrust Act and the ensuing legislation.

In the mid-1970s issues of distribution and access to unique medical resources thrust physicians and especially the department chairs into a much more active position in the medical center and in public. Chairmen found themselves simultaneously engaged in negotiations with hospital administration, members of the Health Services Agencies, and the state mandated certificate of need (CON) administrative bodies. These latter groups would, through resource distribution, fundamentally affect the institutional character of medicine. It now became necessary for chairs to become familiar with sophisticated financial and marketing techniques. At the same time, these CEOs were required to learn about beam hardening, dual energy, DNA transfer, new pharmaceuticals, and reconstruction algorithms. Concerns in quantitative form of risk/benefit, cost/benefit, and relative efficacy started to emerge, and issues of social concern were addressed by chairmen — literally for the first time in medicine.

Biomedical advances in the mid-1970s placed the members of certain departments and ultimately the CEO in new roles for which there was no historical precedent. Chairmen found themselves in an advocacy role for their faculty and in direct competition with fellow chairmen in order to maintain services within their specialty. "Turf" implications of this complexity and intensity had never before been part of the chair's experience. Many had no expertise in negotiations with their medical colleagues or with hospital and institutional administrations regarding these type of issues.

Ethical and moral issues arose that had no historical precedence. For example, the legacy of *Rowe v. Wade* has had far reaching effects in society, and medicine has not been immune. This landmark opinion, recently revisited in Supreme Court hearings, established that a female had the right to make decisions regarding the fate of her own body. This specifically relates to the responsibility and ability to obtain an abortion in the circumstances of an unwanted pregnancy. Implied or attributable to this decision is the right of parents to a "whole" infant at birth. Ultrasound has become so widely applied and the public has been made so aware of its virtues that physicians performing those studies have now been involved in cases seeking compensation under the rubric of "wrongful birth" and "wrongful life." Courtroom exposure and complex depositions associated with these and other cases have become part of the physician's experience which is a new management challenge.

For the past fifteen years and possibly longer, medicine has tended to subspecialization and superspecialization. This phenomenon has evoked and provided sustenance for some of the major advances and has created both challenges and opportunities for the department CEO. From the chairman's viewpoint this subspecialization phenomenon also led to a complete restructuring of staffing patterns and led to internal interaction of the faculty with a different advocacy group. Staff members often became almost exclusively involved in the resource allocation for their section and a departmental posture has become a rarer commodity. Competition for capital equipment and space as well as support staff within the department has become a much more significant issue; these competitions often become interdepartment conflicts.

Abilities in the area of conflict resolution and "people skills" should become the major attributes that search committees emphasize in their choices for chairs. Scholarly accomplishments and clinical preeminence may become of secondary importance. However, credibility within the department and often among the other chairmen still depends on the more traditional areas of assessment, a new variation of the "Peter principle."

The CEO's reputation within the institution for a service department will be judged upon the responsiveness, the efficiency and promptness of the information transfer of studies performed or therapies rendered, and the quality of the individual consultative process. The last will occur in various clinical activities such as "rounds," CPCs, etc. The relationship of these phenomena to resource availability, capacity or quality assurance and non-professional and even professional staffing may not be well understood by the other department leaders or, oftentimes, by hospital and medical school administrations. The department CEO must have skills of persuasion and the abilities to translate a service responsibility into a perceived institutional resource need or needs. The orchestration of the purchase of a cyclotron and a positron emission tomography facility is an example. To do so requires a great deal of independent study to explain the various issues to a Board of Trust, the CON deliberative agency, a state legislature, or even the long range planning group of the institution.

The decision makers often need a great deal of "convincing" to understand why a radiopharmacologist and radiochemist presently employed in a conventional nuclear medicine facility cannot simply take over these new PET duties by becoming more efficient or merely lengthening their working day. How will the PET facility be financially viable? Who should contribute to its initiation? These decision groups often insist upon the actual testimony from the CEO and "responsible" financial officer, the chair. This may be yet another operative expression or extension of the "Peter principle." The budgets for the rather extraordinary capital expenditures in medicine such as $4-6 million for PET require financial sophistication on the part of the CEO. Standard calculations for return on investment for PET often border on the hallucinatory. Amortization of equipment whose technological half life and physical half life might be quite disparate is not for the "faint of spirit" or the uncommitted clinical chair. To agree to make short-lived radiopharmaceuticals for others or to rent cyclotron time to the basic sciences in order to defray operating costs may be an exercise in naivete.

Of course, the CEO may have the ever loyal staff who need the instrumentation, appreciate its virtues and the opportunities it provides and are convinced that the chair, business manager, and administration will handle the financial aspects so well that they, as working staff, will not be encumbered with these details. After all, if there is some reticence on the Board of Trust or institutional administration to enter upon some new venture, one might simply borrow the funds against the departmental escrow account. If there is a temporary (length unknown) "shortfall" from some operational venture one could certainly use escrow funds and later refund the department. Actually, is not the escrow account some external calculation between the Dean of the Medical School, the Vice Chancellor for Health Sciences, and the chairman which can be used for all manner of good works including distributing appropriately proportioned amounts as quarterly, semi-annual, or annual bonuses to the staff?

The chair should have the academic background and experience to fully understand the origin and the implications of the escrow account to be its proper guardian. This is even more crucial than the determination of an appropriate Part A Medicare return or the calculation of institutional overhead for which the chair may also be held accountable. Should the chairperson be trained in business? Knowledge of those specific business issues most important to the discipline will be necessary to effectively interact with the department manager internally and the institution administration, as well as industry, externally.

The chair must understand and establish the role of a mentor and a facilitator for the department. A modern-day chair must encourage his or her staff to be productive and see to it that they garner the recognition for their successful efforts. Opportunities for the staff to serve in the professional organizations and to advance in rank in their parent institution as well as to secure attractive, desirable and competitive positions in others are part of the responsibilities of the position. CEOs can best do this if they have made these types of contributions themselves.

To some physicians, this may have the connotation of "marketing" with some inherently negative reactions that term evokes. However, great departments are made up of great teams and not a single great "titan" at the pinnacle. Sometimes this team process will involve the chair forgoing a personal honor or passing on an opportunity to another staff member. It may mean declining a committee membership as a *quid pro quo* to having one of your faculty included. The chair must be able to recognize these circumstances and have the maturity to realize that over an extended period of time the reward to the department (and often to the chair) will be much greater if they personally demure. Over the years that department chair acting in such a manner will develop the reputation of "someone good to work for." An analogy that is appealing is that of the great athletic coaches whose assistants have also gone on to greatness. Have you ever observed how they over time continue to have great assistant coaches?

Recruitment and replenishment of staff is an ongoing process, and it is greatly facilitated by an historical reputation of a "great place to be or to have been from." The chair must have the grace to take the "long view" with an aggressive and demanding staff because from that clay the medical superstars can be molded. In their role as mentor, chairs should have a set of well articulated convictions. A chair must also be steady and consistent. "Grace under pressure" would be a description we would all aspire to. The consistency displayed by the chair, which can only come with self discipline, should be visible. Behavioral patterns of this type manifested by leaders instills confidence in the faculty.

The chair in an academic department should have a well-recognized expertise in a particular area of the specialty. This should be substantiated by substantive publications in well-recognized journals, possibly a major textbook on the subject, and an internal reputation as a clinical consultant. This image of the chair will be modified over time as the chair must relinquish the clinical leadership role to those that they will support among their faculty. Obviously one cannot properly administrate a department while spending the majority of their time in the clinical area. However, the substantiated belief that the chair at some time made significant clinical and academic contributions and remains capable of doing so will greatly add to the success of the chair's tenure. Respect and credibility within the department are important for any leadership role.

With the institution of a prospective payment system for health care, the department chair in the past several years has been accorded additional responsibilities. Efficiency in the evaluation and treatment process became not just a desirable characteristic of a department but an essential element for financial survival. Over-testing and over-treatment due to subspecialty advocacy has now become an unaffordable luxury. Behavior patterns of long-standing among certain staff members have had to be altered. Chairs must, to a greater extent, ensure that the department is responsive, efficient, and circumspect in selecting the next test, whether or not to perform an additional study, or in choosing the proper therapy. On occasion, the chair will be forced to ask the staff to practice less or to alter practice patterns to avoid those optional activities identified in financial terms as "loss leaders." Even psychiatrists have serious difficulties in having adults change behavioral patterns, but policy makers believe DRGs, HMOs, RAPs, RBRVS and managed care will. The chair must possess new and different skills of persuasion as well as negotiation to approach these challenges.

Although this discourse on the characteristics of a successful department chair has emphasized the multiple skills required and the complexities of the position, it is not time to call for the *dies irae*, the traditional chant for the dead, because the rewards of the position are many. If CEOs exercise the appropriate amount of self discipline, they can continue to enjoy the personal pleasure of their contributions. Discipline also provides the feeling of control and adds greatly to one's concept of self worth. A department CEO is, in this instance, a very desirable position. As an indicator, for every available chairmanship there are legions of candidates. In fact, many can only take solace in Matthew 22:1-14, "For many are called but few are chosen."

Chapter 20

THE ADMINISTRATION OF STAFF ENRICHMENT TIME

Logic would dictate that staff in medicine would have a significant amount of their usual activities devoted to personal pursuits. This is an implicit aim in most institutions and an explicit goal in some. What is meant by the concept of this time and the organizational and administrative measures designed to effect this objective provide a very interesting challenge in the current medical environment.

A wide diversity among the various implications and perceptions of time exists between the medical unit leadership, staff, support colleagues, and institutional governance bodies at all levels. In some departments, discretionary time is regarded as a luxury, while in others it is treated as a divine right. Much of the rhetoric emanating from staff discussions of discretionary time arises from a lack of clarity by the leadership as to what is the expected result of this time, how that product will be quantitated, and the consequences of lack of institutional benefit or, conversely, the rewards of appropriate productivity.

In my department, discretionary time relates to the opportunity to pursue personal goals. Implicit in this effort was the generation of a defined plan for the effort, a funding mechanism for the project (if appropriate), and a strategy to complete and share the results in a timely fashion.

How should the administrator decide on the amount of time to allocate for each staff member? The easiest system of all would be to award each member a fixed amount, such as 20 percent of the work week, for personal time. Essentially, each staff member in this system would have one day a week to pursue their own activities. I do not believe that this system either encourages productive activities or fosters general progress for the institution. My experience has been that staff members tend to misuse the time, in that this period is often devoted to mundane personal rather than professional activities if there is no accountability. I suggest that an annual review of each staff member's productivity be undertaken and that each be counselled on at least an annual basis.

There will be some staff members who are undeniably productive for the institution, and these will often have significant extramural return as well. Possibly, their discretionary time should be increased to greater than 20 percent.

Alternatively, there will be other staff who initially have little or nothing in terms of creative inclinations. They should be encouraged to engage in productive activities, and their time should eventually be accordingly reduced if there is no evidence of change. In this context, over time, these staff members should be encouraged to choose a service track with respect to their progress in the institution.

The essential ingredient to make this administrative technique successful is the development of a clear-cut guideline by the leadership as to what is expected of discretionary time. This time should be evaluated in the context of defined productivity. As long as the parameters and guidelines are known in advance, and as long as the staff considers them to be fair, there should be relatively little resistance to accountability and use of the arrangement outlined. Tacit in this discussion is the implication that resources will be available.

The administrative challenge in the era of the 1970's and 80's was to create the space, technology and financial resources and then motivate the staff. There were so many positive aspects to this endeavor that, while it has many of the characteristics of a challenge, it had very few earmarks of a problem. The staff had the perspective of formerly having little or no facilities to now enjoying the possibility of having adequate resources for their activities. The members of the staff had been a significant part of the process through which these unique and valuable assets were added to the department. Many members of the staff might very well take pride in the presence of these resources even though they did not personally use them. There is an inherent mandate in newness and a quality of attractive naivete in the realization that you now have an intellectual opportunity because some resource has been recently placed at their disposal.

With the advent of the 1990's, allocation of these resources (especially time) has become a significant issue, raising concerns of equity and fairness. Staff will begin utilizing resources that require a great deal more rigor with regard to time and organization than former endeavors. In fact, thc very nature of this type of activity will come to require the administration of the necessary resources including time. Accountability has also become a requisite ingredient in this management issue.

Concomitant with the changing requirements and motivation of the staff have been increased clinical demands. The latter phenomenon is certainly not unique to any discipline but has been visited upon all of medicine. The implications upon staff time in general have been an erosion of the non-service component in favor of income-producing activities. There are many institutional incentives to generate additional monies from clinical work.

Discretionary time has now become a more precious commodity and, in some institutions, a *cause celebre*. Must discretionary time produce awards and garner acclaim for the institution, as I have suggested? In the present societal environment of accountability, are these not reasonable expectations? Conventional wisdom is that this "free (discretionary) time" may be the *quid pro quo* for decreased monetary compensation. I believe that this is true only if there is measurable productivity over some reasonable time period. The commonly held notion that discretionary time is a substitute for increased salaries is a perversion of the intent of the goal of discretionary time.

At the least, staff members who are using discretionary time as an extra day off for pursuit of recreational needs should be counseled on the intent of the discretionary time concept. If such individuals continue to improperly use the resource, they should be persuaded to pursue a clinical track with full-time service and teaching responsibilities. The message needs to be made clear that discretionary professional time is for professional pursuits; if the system is misused, it will soon be recognized by the entire institution. One should convey the idea (especially to young staff) that it is a privilege and responsibility to be involved in these activities.

I believe that the administration of the institution must make substantial efforts to have the medical staff recognize the implied responsibility for discretionary time. The process must be somewhat performance-oriented. This time is a resource, not just a reward. It may be granted initially by the institution, but after some reasonable time the continuation should be in response to some perceived benefit. Rigid criteria should not be confused with those reflecting rigor. Some accountability must exist, but how it is to be administered will vary. Institutions with senior leadership who have reputations for fairness and experience will be able to use these staff members as an acceptable monitoring group. Those institutions which do not have such people on their staff should have a much more democratic system. However, whatever the mechanism, there must be a sense of accountability and a perception of responsibility. The concept and allocation of discretionary professional time will be an even more important management issue for the 1990s than it has been in the past decades.

Chapter 21

THE PHILOSOPHY OF ACQUIRING MEDICAL RESOURCES

The escalation of health care costs has markedly increased public awareness of expenditures in every component of this complicated mix. Particular attention has been directed to medical technology and for very appropriate reasons, including high costs, extensive publicity in the lay literature, and the addiction of clinical colleagues to the use of these facilities.

Regulation has been attempted from every sector. Public policies, legislative enactments, and economic disincentives have been employed to address the increase of health care expenditures that relate to medical technology. Medicine has been significantly affected in the last two decades by such measures as certificates of need (CON); antitrust interpretations following the 1974 Goldfarb decision; and the FTC, HCFA, OTA, as well as FDA decisions and opinions. We have seen the imposition of diagnosis related groups (DRGs) and, more recently, the resource-based relative value scale (RBRVS) and now managed care. The present administration is considering price controls and managed care to control costs. However, the so called "competitive model" has avid proponents especially among the medical establishment. In considering technology, there also remains the impending threat of present and proposed legislation as well as the decision of the Inspector General's office regarding physician owned centers. This heavily regulated and everchanging environment increases the complexity of medical technology acquisition. While the answers and solutions will predictably change, certain present observations may have validity and prove interesting.

In the past few years, I have been concerned with the acquisition of a number of the more costly and sophisticated imaging devices: a cyclotron/PET facility, several MRIs, x-ray computed CTs, and digital angiographic suites. These have required different strategies, but several general suggestions should be offered:

1) Involve the staff that will use the technology.
2) Bundle the acquisitions if possible.
3) For a new capability or service, coordinate with an institutional plan for growth.

4) Inform the clinical staff and assess their level of support. Also, elicit and enhance their support.
5) Identify the decision makers early in the process. Advisors and decision makers should know their role with certainty.

Several comments regarding these guidelines above might be helpful. By combining the expertise of your technical scientists and the staff who will utilize the equipment, one can obtain a reasonably accurate characterization of the technology. When manufacturers find that their initial encounter will be with these teams, they will send their appropriate scientists and technical people. This will obviate the inefficient and embarrassing scene where the MBA/marketing representative is asked by the potential acquirers technical questions or design specifications for which he does not and should not know the answers.

The technical analysis may require a visit to the manufacturer's plant or, if the instrumentation acquisition involves a prototype machine, to the research facility. By beginning the acquisition in this manner, one can get some idea of the availability of the scientific expertise of the manufacturer. In every organization that purveys high technology there is an "answer man." You need to find out who and where this person is before acquiring a technology from that particular manufacturer.

After having arrived at a consensus on the technological possibilities for the acquisition, the team should then look at the manufacturer from another perspective. Often, instead of clear, outright winners on technology there are trade-offs. If this is the circumstance, then the two parameters that become most important are: 1) the position of the manufacturer in the industry and 2) the company's service record.

Every industry has leaders who maintain standards by which others are judged. Medical technology in the last several decades, however, has been rather volatile commercially, with companies moving in and out of the field. Some companies failed because this technology was not a line of business with which they were familiar. Many of these companies had accumulated a large body of assets by manufacturing products quite unrelated to medical technology and had served a completely different group of consumers. For these reasons, they had acquired the financial assets to enter the medical instrument field but should not have because they did not have the expertise. When these companies realized that the new line featuring medical technology was a "loss leader" and did not enhance the consumer's perception of their other products, they abandoned the field.

Once, acting as a consultant for a very affluent drug company, I was told that the same marketing techniques which had allowed the company to lead the industry in the sale of potions and pills could be successful in marketing a body CT scanner. Upon objecting to that analogy, I was also informed that "toothbrushes and CAT scanners are bought for the same reason; you make people want them." If all other considerations are equal, purchase equipment from a company that is primarily in the instrumentation business. The fate of that company? They were out of the medical business in three years.

You may already have a very good assessment of the service reliability of the company from your previous experience with other instrumentation they manufacture. Although dealing with small start-up companies gives one a personal stake in the relationship and is accompanied by a spirit of adventure, it can shortly turn to a misadventure because of difficulties in service. Most of the time the fledgling company does not have the personnel to meet the challenge. Small companies have difficulty predicting their growth and also lack the cash flow to stockpile these skilled and somewhat rare individuals. Rarely, if the small company has a clear and important technological lead over the others, we will negotiate to become a test and demonstration site — hopefully *the* site.

Small companies, in order to penetrate a market or to have instrumentation at a certain institution, will offer significant financial inducements. This may be a false savings: downtime will not only prove very expensive for the short-term but will have long-term results, as it can significantly alter clinician perception of reliability and responsiveness and change referral patterns.

To cite an example from personal experience, my x-ray CT units did not have as good an algorithm for absorption correction to display the soft tissues of the head and neck as those of another manufacturer's CT located in a nearby competing hospital. Our own otolaryngology department began referring their studies to the other hospital, and even when our CT instrumentation was upgraded it required considerable internal marketing to recapture that patient population. In my opinion, "downtime" is the most tragic undercalculation in the technology planning process. Simply accounting the overhead and immediate lost revenue markedly underestimates the effect of downtime. Avoid the devil, death and downtime—possibly not even in that order.

Another consideration regarding service is the very expensive contracts which are fairly difficult for the individual institution to evaluate. Your MBAs and the like in financial management may be able to offer some industry standard, especially in regards to pricing. However, the quality of the service is what you want to determine. Many times you will ask your counterparts at other institutions if they have had experience with this particular manufacturer and what the experience was. As you know, leopards have difficulty...

In our institution we have had an extensive quality assurance program funded largely by Part A reimbursement. We have a number of scientists in our employ, but at the same time we have very expensive service contracts for our complex instrumentation. We are constantly exploring with the instrument manufacturers which maintenance and corrective procedures could be performed "in house" without violating various warranty and service agreements. This is an area where the acquirer should obtain as good an agreement prior to the first payment as possible, because there is very little chance that the circumstance will improve later. We have found that often neither the manufacturer nor the acquiring medical group matches the service contract with the number of hours the instrument is in daily use. For example, if the MRI operates two 8-hour shifts, this should be reflected in the service contract and the risk calculated for 16 hours.

Another vague area in present considerations of capital equipment acquisition comes under the general rubric of "buy outs." In days of yore, we had standard amortization tables and knew when mechanical obsolescence would allow us to replace a machine that was virtually worthless — the "used TV" equivalent. Now the risk of technological obsolescence is so great that we can only hope that our technology has not reached this state before we get past all the hurdles that will allow us to acquire it. What determines technological obsolescence? Is it when the instrument performance is inferior to those from competing hospitals? Might it be when the procedure time is "too long"? Or is it when the manufacturer has invested so heavily in a different instrumentation that replacement parts and service technologists are not readily available? Could it be when downtime and service bills have rendered the unit a cost center only?

Once you have decided that in your environment you must replace a particular technology, you are now faced with the problem of determining the present market value of the instrument you have. This, then, becomes a negotiation between your institution (hopefully represented by you) and the manufacturer. Unfortunately, there is insufficient experience in the financial community to simply read this from a standardized table. The manufacturer may have very little experience in the secondary market for your machine, which, after all, they may have been manufacturing for only a few years. If there has been a quantum leap in the improvement of instrumentation, then the discussion may turn to "a third or even fourth world country" or a charitable deduction. Thus, one must *a priori* make some general evaluation as to the expected technological life of the instrument to be acquired. This estimate will also be helpful when making more specific- decisionsconcerning leasing time or length of any proposed loan.

The needs and resources of institutions are so variable that discussion of any specific financing arrangements would have limited applicability. However, I believe it is important to have an agreement that the holder of the loan or lease will remain the same as the financial entity on the initial contract. This will usually ensure that the administrator can have a personal relationship with the lender. Loans from the vendor have this particular advantage.

While the risks in the acquisition of sophisticated instrumentation are greater today than they have ever been, the needs are also greater. Clinicians, as advocates for their patients, often demand the availability of a particular capability or service. Service specialties should exploit this perceived need by having these colleagues articulate their wishes to the decision makers in the institution. However, this activity is not without risk and a true consensus is preferable. The methodology to achieve this end will be discussed subsequently.

Chapter 22

CAPITAL EXPENDITURES: PROCUREMENT OF TECHNOLOGY THROUGH THE CONSENSUS DEVELOPMENT PROCESS

Institutional expenditures for the technology component of health care delivery have received great attention because of their visibility and the perception that they significantly increase costs. This has led to an increased accountability and pre-acquisition justification. However, often the data requested is preliminary, incomplete, and is only available from a variety of sources. Preparing an adequate, well-justified proposal may pose undue and possibly unnecessary hardship upon the administrative leadership of the institution. To fail to do this in the past, however, has resulted in the acquisition of expensive and costly technology by institutions or the purchase of costly equipment utilizing institutional resources without a unanimity of opinion to do so. Certain of these difficulties might be obviated by the treatment of the process as a consensus conference.

A consensus conference, as defined by the U.S. Office of Medical Applications Research (OMAR) of the National Institutes of Health (NIH), is a technique employed to evaluate the available scientific information regarding a biomedical technology and to produce a consensus document reflecting general agreement on the knowledge base coupled with the opinions of those involved. It is essential, however, that the document include dissenting views, although such views have infrequently been represented in the NIH consensus reports. This methodology is viewed as a relatively inexpensive and timely mechanism to evaluate the different attributes of a medical technology determining its relative safety, efficiency, and efficacy. While the Consensus Development Program of the NIH limits itself primarily to issues of safety and efficacy and largely excludes social, economic, and ethical considerations, its application at an institutional level is not obliged to do so.

The chief advantage of this technique is that it can involve all of the responsible groups in the acquisition of information, distribution of evidence, and sharing more equitably in the decision process. In the preparation, a reasonable body of research and prior utilization, if available, will be acquired prior to the deliberative effort. Ideally, this should be distributed so as to bring to the attention of all parties what potential alternatives might exist rather than have competing groups present their data to foster a certain line of reasoning leading to a favorable outcome for a particular group.

In order to eliminate either the deliberative or unintended bias in a literature search and preparation, this task should be the province of a disinterested party - often a staff person reporting to the administration of the institution. This effort should result in a summary of each main body of knowledge in the literature and a statement that explicitly expresses the criteria for evaluation of the quality of the studies. A synthesis of the literature using meta-analysis should be employed wherever appropriate. The body of data should represent a compilation of articles related to efficacy and effectiveness of the technology and the consequences if there is a modification of practice employing that technology. Contained therein should be any adverse effects to the patient population and the institution related to that technology. In the instance of noninvasive technologies (generally regarded as "safe"), the consequences of false-positive and false-negative diagnoses should be emphasized. Not only are literature searches useful in deliberations regarding technology acquisition, but tradition and experience suggest that this valuable technique has not been a part of the process as reflected by the literature itself.

A systematic review of articles published in the leading four journals reporting the various aspects of ultrasound in obstetrics revealed the following mix. Of 182 articles cited, 132 were related to the diagnostic value of the procedure, 14 were concerned with the effects on practice patterns, and only 9 addressed the issue of the effect of ultrasound on the health of the patients. The major determinant leading to the acquisition of this technology seems to be the diagnostic value of the procedure and not the broader and more complex assessment of the effect upon the health of the potential population.

In defining the appropriateness of and the outcomes of the use of a technology, it often appears difficult to be explicit, especially if the technology is complex and new. Appropriateness for a magnetic resonance imaging (MRI) scanner, for example, could be viewed in terms of cost/benefit, cost effectiveness, and risk/benefit analysis, but how would one factor in a "dynamic imaging" package or the choice of a 1.5 vs a 0.05 T magnet? Outcomes should be determined for each patient population group, but the long- and short-term outcomes may be different. In the development of any informed consensus, there is always a disparity between the goal that may be set and the information to base the decisions leading to that outcome if one is dealing with rapidly advancing technology. By constructing an unbiased synthesis of what is known, the best approximation could nonetheless be obtained. The common ground provided by the synthesis is particularly important for the lay persons and basic scientists involved in the process of acquiring medical technology for an institution. This synthesis provides a way of determining not only that which is known but also that which has not been determined about a particular technology, providing the institution some idea about the financial and other risks that they may be undertaking. A decision whether to embark upon the costly adventure of a cyclotron/positron emission tomography (PET) facility involves definite financial risks to institutions, as both value to patient health and expectations for compensation from clinical procedures are relatively unknown at present.

As was implied from the literature search regarding early clinical evaluations of MRI, studies supporting the use of that technology were based upon data obtained from what has been judged by some as poorly conducted studies. However, this circumstance is often quite apparent from the pre-acquisition literature search and is, in itself, useful. The synthesis of the literature also provides a systematic way of identifying experts in the field who may subsequently act as useful consultants during the deliberation process. The informed network approach that is customarily employed in this activity has a greater tendency for bias and is less scientifically defensible than the two-tiered process outlined.

The relating of each consensus statement regarding subsequent capital expenditure acquisitions to the scientific bases for the decision makes it clear whether they may have been based upon clinical trials, epidemiological studies, clinical observations organized to evaluate outcomes, or primarily upon expert opinions. This methodology allows the decision-making group to formulate the justification process, stating the degree of certainty inferred from the determinative data. As institutions will be increasingly accountable for their decisions regarding capital expenditures, this may be of greater future importance.

One might dismiss this process as unduly formal and conclude that the present informal methodology has traditionally worked well. The historical group process might well be enhanced, however, if the decision makers could limit most of their discussions to such useful considerations as the probabilities of positive and negative outcomes from the use of the proposed technology and the patient utility associated with those outcomes. Having all of the participants begin with a respectable body of knowledge and the consensus process initiated by an unbiased or relatively unbiased participant will obviate the fiduciary roles of the most interested parties and should reduce the rhetoric involved in natural issues of "turf."

Consensus should not be equated with unanimity, but some less restrictive definition of the goal of the process should be adopted. One may move toward a consensus by polling (anonymously or publicly) the group and by the use of a rating technique as one moves forward through the process. Complicated medical technology has an inherent complexity that may make some qualification of one's choices entirely appropriate. The RAND/UCLA modification of the NIH consensus procedures rates choices in order to facilitate arriving at a consensus and later to document the process. This information can be subsequently employed to suggest a hierarchy or degree of certitude for the recommendations of acquisition.

Shortly after a consensus is arrived at, a document indicating the choices and justification of the decisions should be produced. Timeliness will facilitate the action flowing from the consensus and will assist in recording accurately the agreements reached and the reasons for these agreements. Some medical policy groups have attempted to expedite the process by providing the consensus panel the literature search prior to the deliberations and even go so far as to draft a preliminary consensus statement. Panelists may be asked to rate the indications to determine the appropriate choice of technology in advance, using a modified Delphi method. However, in deliberations of capital equipment acquisitions, I believe that this does not allow sufficient analysis of the data that is often available.

Health care organizations are commonly involved in the acquisition and financing of medical technology. A consensus approach may allow us to better clarify the nature of the interaction between the attributes and limitations of the technology being diffused, the characteristics of the adopting institutions, the expected changes in patient outcomes, and the social and economic context of the environment in which the technology will be employed.

ACKNOWLEDGEMENT

The thoughts of my colleague Seymour Perry were especially helpful in preparing this chapter.

Chapter 23

MANAGEMENT OF PRACTICE GUIDELINES: EFFECT ON MALPRACTICE CLAIMS FOR THE MEDICAL ADMINISTRATOR

Of the many initiatives to reduce medical costs while providing quality medical care, practice guidelines have been proposed as a measure that might assist with many of the perceived difficulties. These suggested patterns of physician behavior can be viewed from several perspectives.

Guidelines are now appearing as instructions for medical applications and have been proposed by policy makers to change practice styles and reduce inappropriate or unnecessary diagnostic and therapeutic procedures to decrease costs. Can practice guidelines also be expected to reduce the malpractice claims and the transactional costs associated with malpractice litigation?

Because malpractice costs are perceived by policy makers to represent a significant financial problem, practice guidelines have also been proposed to streamline the process of settling medical malpractice claims. Malpractice premiums in most states remain high and the direct costs of the malpractice process itself can be measured by the size of these premiums, which are now believed to be as high as $7 billion annually. However, this incompletely characterizes the problem because the indirect and hidden costs of the malpractice system may be many times the direct costs of the insurance.

The current health care system contributes to heightened patient expectations, which are individualized. Untoward outcomes are often believed to be *de facto* caused by provider error rather than underlying health problems. Injured patients are often not currently recompensed in a timely manner, leading to consumer frustration. Some believe that the costs of malpractice litigation might not be of great concern if they were offset by efficient compensation for those who are injured. Could this be achieved with properly formulated practice guidelines? Malpractice litigation, at present, is not an efficient cost-spreading mechanism. One reason is that the majority of funds eventually are absorbed by administrative costs unlike other means of compensation for injury.

If authoritative criteria were available, could they serve as the guideline to evaluate the performance of an individual physician? If these guidelines were developed pluralistically, might physicians, third party payors, and consumers still have the choice of alternative standards to characterize their relationship? Would the proposed guidelines subsequently be viewed as prescriptive standards to assign provider fault? Is the present tort system defensible as an effective mechanism to ensure quality assurance, especially in an area such as medical technology? Does our legal system work to appropriately compensate the injured and serve as an effective deterrent of medical negligence? These are important issues that the medical administrator must address.

Problems with the litigation process have led to demands for alternative methods for presenting scientific evidence in courts. The standard of care is only implicit in the verdict of a lay jury. This is often based upon a decision after hearing subjective expert medical testimony that is often confusing and conflicting. Suggested solutions range from establishing or embellishing pretrial screening methods, limiting the size of malpractice awards and attorneys' fees, as well as regulating the qualifications of expert medical witnesses. Others have suggested a no-fault system or an administrative process outside the civil justice system.

It is difficult to justify the legal system's reliance upon customary and usual practices as the standard for appropriate physician behavior. Many physicians also object to this methodology, because it is perceived as vague and imprecise, exposing them to malpractice liability in an entirely unpredictable manner as standard of care in medicine may change with each significant innovation.

Many believe that practice guidelines will have the same role as medical reference books, articles in medical journals, or research studies as evidence of the standard of care. There would be little or no reduction in the time expended in the process or in the expense of malpractice litigation. Others expect explicit practice guidelines to even increase the number of claims filed.

Practice guidelines will be systematically developed only as recommendations but could be made binding for physicians by converting them into statutes or regulations. Guidelines should, however, rarely even purport to be probative of custom as such and would only constitute hearsay evidence. Guidelines formed by a pluralistic or consensus method by generally recognized medical organizations under the federally mandated guidelines program might become the object of judicial notice, obviating certain forms of expert testimony.

Development of medical guidelines is a significant cultural departure from almost complete reliance upon professional judgment. The need for standards in terms of administrative accountability to the payors (private insurers, corporations, and government) has encouraged the development of some form of reference guidelines. Guidelines without a different intent, however, for the clinical practice of medicine in the United States have actually been developed over fifty years. Many physician organizations have developed their own practice parameters and are presently extending and updating them.

Public interest in practice guidelines is underscored by the mandate from Congress in November 1989 for the Agency for Health Care Policy and Research (AHCPR) to develop, evaluate, and disseminate practice guidelines. Under this aegis, practice guidelines will be published by the Forum for Quality and Effectiveness in Health Care. Interest in practice guidelines has grown because many believe they offer the potential to simultaneously control health care costs and improve quality. They could enfranchise consumers to choose the style of medical care they prefer. Insurers, health maintenance organizations, and utilization management firms are moving toward using practice guidelines as the basis for regularizing coverage and bring order to payment decisions. Practice guidelines could, in malpractice cases, replace community standards with the judgement criteria set by guidelines. This is not as important a departure as one might perceive, for specialty standards are largely national.

Our system for resolving medical malpractice disputes through the legal system requires that the patient's injury was caused by negligent actions of the physician be established. Generally, the claim of negligence involves determining whether the provider adhered to some generally agreed upon standard of care. Standards of care are usually determined by a jury, based on evidence provided and precedent decisions about the prevailing care in the community — whether geographic or based upon like practitioners of that discipline. Courts have sometimes been accused of substituting standards of their own creation rather than those emanating from professional societies. The practice guideline movement could diminish this alleged phenomenon. "Community" has been increasingly interpreted in a regional or national context because of increased access to medical information but in areas of medical innovation there may be little agreement.

There is a perception that a diluted locality rule results in increased litigation because it subjects the practitioners to more imprecise guidelines of conduct. A number of states have attempted to restate the standard of care by reference to local practice. The courts have continued to insist that deviation from standard medical practice is the legal justification for a verdict of liability. Expert testimony must demonstrate that the health care provider departed from the prevailing level of care. Guidelines in theory may obviate this process.

The process described might also be expedited if expert testimony is limited to supplementing practice guidelines as proof of the standard of care. Plaintiffs could only be required to demonstrate that guidelines which properly apply to their case were not followed. Defendants might argue that the appropriate guidelines were followed and that the plaintiff introduced inappropriate guidelines or that certain guidelines had become obsolete.

Practice guidelines might reduce the number and expense of malpractice cases by prospectively altering physician behavior. If practice guidelines were appropriate and followed, the quality of care might be improved and fewer claims filed and spurious claims reduced if more explicit guidelines about appropriate care were formulated. Attorneys could better evaluate whether negligence has occurred and whether the facts in a case have merit.

If physicians adhere to the guidelines, will they be absolved from the responsibility of an untoward event? Legal proceedings may be expedited and less costly through the use of a common standard of care. Rather than establish the standard of care, the legal process could focus upon whether extenuating circumstances mitigated against the application of the standard in a particular case. The reasonableness of the physician's action might be evaluated in lay terms rather than from an entirely medical perspective through the use of practice guidelines.

On the other hand, practice guidelines could cause the number of malpractice claims to increase. Many believe that there are many more injuries resulting from professional negligence than there are claims filed. Practice guidelines that are consistent, comprehensive, and well accepted may allow better evaluation of these missed cases leading to allegations of malpractice. If guidelines serve to define malpractice more precisely, some meritorious cases that are not currently pursued could be identified.

For practice guidelines to exert any influence on the number of claims or cost of settling malpractice claims, they must be developed for procedures that frequently lead to negligence claims. Practice guidelines should be widely accepted and fully integrated into clinical medical practice and readily understood to be interpreted in a litigation setting. New areas in medicine should not become standards until they have achieved this status. If claims are filed for adverse outcomes involving medical events for which guidelines have been developed, these should be related to the adverse event and each malpractice claim to a specific medical procedure. The trier of fact should determine if the appropriate practice guideline was followed and, if not, evaluate whether the use of the guideline might have averted the adverse event.

Most policy makers contend that available guidelines could provide useful inculpatory or exculpatory evidence for about 20% of medical injuries at present. In order for practice guidelines to be used as a standard of care in malpractice cases, they should be widely accepted by the courts and the legal system. Professional societies should endorse practice guidelines that are of high quality so that they could be used by administrators to manage their areas of responsibility.

Recognizing the need to base practice guidelines on rigorous clinical research and soundly generated professional consensus, the AHCPR is investing significant resources in guidelines development. Specialty groups will do, or have already done, likewise. These major efforts should improve the future quality of practice guidelines.

Practice guidelines are not to be formulas for practice but should fit the specific circumstances of practice. Unlike standards that are applied rigidly and followed, guidelines will be flexible, allowing choices and alternatives for physicians and patients. Deviations from guidelines will not necessarily imply malpractice, nor will adherence to guidelines obviate one from legal challenge. If a guideline is widely publicized and accepted, the "respected minority" doctrine could still be exculpatory for providers who have not followed the guideline for that particular clinical circumstance.

If negligence is claimed, medical experts will be necessary to establish that a particular practice guideline is authoritative or to argue that the practice guideline is not applicable. However, guidelines should give the tort system an improved benchmark to judge the appropriateness of physician conduct.

Interest in the development and implementation of practice guidelines may lead to the establishment of a formal dialogue between purveyors and consumers about the quality of care. This activity should aid in the setting of proper national standards. Practice guidelines could also assist in the proper adoption of medical innovations and technology. As practice guidelines are developed and promulgated, health care costs could decrease because of fewer unnecessary diagnostic procedures. Medical standards could also be increasingly codified by practice guidelines, allowing a much improved and accepted standard of care.

Dispute resolution following guideline adoption could be accomplished through the use of prior agreements about the nature of claims to be adjudicated and use of neutral arbitrators. The courts have traditionally accepted such agreements in general terms. These guidelines could be integrated into such agreements by specifying that they would provide the basis for determination of liability. This could streamline the arbitration process and further reduce costs associated with dispute resolution. Tort law, as applied to medical malpractice, in its present form has over-regulated and, at times, ill treated medical practice. Evolving in a pluralistic fashion, based upon well-funded activities in outcomes and effectiveness research, practice guidelines might facilitate the deregulation of medicine and increase consumer choice.

The introduction of practice guidelines into the current malpractice system may not initially reduce the number of malpractice claims filed or even the cost of settling those claims immediately. However, these caveats may be obviated by the expected progress. The challenge in medical administration is to respond to the factor of change. This movement will become increasingly appropriate as we journey along the path of managed care.

ACKNOWLEDGMENT

I am grateful to the assistants of the legal staff of the AMA and to my colleague Clark Hauighurst in the preparation of this chapter.

Chapter 24

THE ADMINISTRATION OF EXCLUSIVE CONTRACTS: ARE THEY FOR PUBLIC BENEFIT?

Exclusive contracts for medical services have been popular since the 1980s for a variety of reasons. Among those chiefly cited are allocative efficiency, scheduling benefit, quality control, and the avoidance of resource duplication. Often, contracts are utilized to secure and maintain a particular service or activity felt to be necessary for the conduct of a business or to ensure its existence for the public good.

Medical economists have reasoned that health care institutions, by contracting with a single professional or professional group, could ensure that the service would be continuously available for the period of the contract. Under this arrangement, the institution might acquire medical services which would all be performed by the same professional group. This is believed to represent the most appropriate strategy to exercise quality control, avoid the perils of physician self-referral, and expedite patient care.

Also, under this exclusive contract, the sophisticated and expensive technology would be situated in a single locus and presumably be more readily available for patients. Support personnel for this enterprise could be in one location, reducing overhead costs for the infrastructure necessary to maintain what has traditionally proven to be a costly and rather complex operation. Since the multiple alternatives of diagnosis and treatment were available to the contracting professional groups, they would presumably be more likely to choose the most efficacious ones and not "overtest" or "overtreat" either through naivete or design.

Physicians receiving these contracts in the early to mid 1980s, due to the compensation methodologies at that time, were encouraged to submit a separate charge from the institutional one. Hence, patient services were compensated by the method and rubric of "technical fee" and "professional fee." The professional groups, having secured the exclusive contract for a defined service, were able to plan their activities in an organized manner, acquire staff in a predictable fashion, and exercise quality control of support personnel. Among their professional groups, in a reasonably effective manner, they could maintain control over the facility, in general, according to the dictates of their conscience regarding standards of practice. Members in the institution, principally the clinicians, generally supported this arrangement because of the scheduling benefit to their patients and because they enjoyed the convenience and efficiency of dealing with a single professional group.

The litany of benefits just cited does not mean that this type of exclusive arrangement was universally accepted without legal challenge. Among the most widely known of these were *Hyde v Jefferson Parish*, *White v. Rockingham Radiologists*, *Konik v. Champlain Valley* and *Coastal Neuropsychiatric Associates. P.A. et al. v. Onslow Memorial Hospital Inc.* Generally, these precedent cases represent a challenge to an exclusive contractual arrangement by which a physician or group of physicians are denied access to or the use of a perceived scarce resource by the terms of the exclusive contractual arrangement between the institution and another professional group. Before examining the role of the CEO, several of these cases, through analysis, might provide us with insights leading to an appropriate management strategy.

In *White v. Rockingham Radiologists*, the plaintiff, a neurologist, wished to perform and interpret x-ray computed tomographic (CT) studies on his patients utilizing technology placed in a particular hospital but owned by an investment group. The exclusive contractual arrangement of the hospital with the Rockingham Radiology group precluded Dr. White from interpreting these diagnostic studies and being compensated for this service. White sued, alleging a tying arrangement between the hospital and the Rockingham group, a group boycott as a *per se* violation of antitrust, and denial of access to the marketplace compromising his professional activities and, tacitly, the potential advantages to his patients. The courts upheld the exclusive contracts in *White* and the other cases by citing those reasons which have been noted above. Exclusive contracts for medical services have withstood the challenges not only of physicians within the system but the combination of certificates of need (CON) which limited widespread distribution of their expensive technology, the changes in granting of hospital privileges, and the access barrier due to these legal arrangements.

Hospital privileges have historically been granted to physicians upon application by a process that reflected the compassion that physicians had for other members of their profession and the control they exercised in the process. Following the *Darling v. Charleston Community Hospital* landmark case, it became apparent that the ultimate responsibility for the activity of these physicians who had privileges in a particular hospital might well reside in the hospital board of trust, and the methodology and intent of the privileges granting changed dramatically. CEOs of medical institutions responded promptly.

The bylaws of many hospitals were rewritten to impose a strict and rigorous process whereby physicians could secure privileges in hospitals only after meeting substantial challenges to their education and experience. Also, the revisions of hospital bylaws provided for a much more defined methodology for the withdrawal of privileges and the removal of physicians from the medical staff. These changes provided little discomfort because administrators and practicing physicians seemed to sense its importance and necessity.

Hospital privileges became more difficult to obtain, and more defined responsibilities and professional quality control were required for their maintenance. Another unnoted or at least little appreciated facet occurred, the division or separation of hospital privileges, which were administered by the professional staff, and the exclusive contracts for services, which were under the control of the administration of the institution. While, in theory, these two groups (administrators and physicians) have the same goals, i.e., patient welfare, their mandate and motivation are often quite different. The professional staff must ensure standard of care and maintain quality control. The institutional administration must ensure financial viability. Thus, one is a professional competence mandate, whereas the other is an economic mandate. While these generally may be in accord, certain external events may very well place the two groups in significant conflict. Management of this fundamental difference is an administrative challenge.

The various initiatives in recent years to limit the spiraling costs of medical care have changed the climate wherein separation of technical and professional charges were almost universally encouraged. As hospital incomes were decreased by many of these, compensation formulas and changing patient mix concomitant with increased costs and overhead, the number of institutional profit centers diminished. However, in many health care facilities, the professional compensation of the medical groups remained stable or may have increased with the institution of new services. Hospital management companies and individual health care facilities began to view the proceeds from these exclusive contractual arrangements as potential sources for revenue. At least two methodologies have been employed to effect the changes felt necessary for the administrators to assist institutional viability. The first is simply to contract with another group at a significantly lower rate for professional compensation, eliminating fee for service or effectively removing this methodology of billing altogether. Upon challenge of antitrust, management companies and hospitals have simply utilized sufficient time and money to withstand a valid legal challenge and impose their group upon the institution. By continued legal delays and often a series of appeals, they may well exceed the financial resources the plaintiff physician or medical group can make available. Physicians have an aversion to the legal system, and expecting one's colleagues to become colitigants is not realistic so the members with the exclusive contract must self finance the legal challenge leveled at the management group.

A much more effective ploy to void an unwanted exclusive contract has been employed recently and is illustrated by what many feel will be a landmark case. In *Lewisburg Community Hospital. Inc. v. David Alfredson, M.D.*, the radiologist had a five-year exclusive contractual arrangement to utilize the instrumentation of that facility to perform and interpret all imaging studies and separately charge a professional fee for services. The plaintiff, Alfredson, had staff privileges granted by the professional board of the hospital. In the hospital bylaws, there was a provision giving physicians whose privileges were withdrawn the right to a hearing which would require the institution to show cause for the action voiding staff privileges. However, Alfredson's exclusive contract had been terminated by the management firm, and the professional board of the hospital was not a party to that action. Thus, Alfredson's staff appointment to the hospital remained intact, but he was now denied use of the facilities. Obviously, with removal of access to the technology, Alfredson's ability to perform and interpret imaging procedures, for all intents and purposes, was voided; thus, he was tacitly denied the marketplace for which he was specifically trained and presumably skilled. Despite some rather discouraging precedent decisions in favor of hospital management, the physician sought relief in the courts.

Upon challenge of their act, the hospital and management company pleaded that they had made a purely economic and administrative decision regarding a business contract for services - not unlike many other contractual arrangements which institutions must enter into as a natural consequence of conducting business. They chose not to address the issue of whether or not Alfredson's ability to practice in the hospital, secured by his staff privileges, had been significantly reduced.

The fundamental principle at issue in this and other related cases is whether or not the administrative entity given the responsibility to conduct the financial matters of the institution can make economic decisions that significantly impact the quality of patient care without some overseer activity of the professional leadership. Stated differently, can a physician's professional privileges ensure their ability to practice their particular discipline of medicine, or might they be precluded from doing so by having their access to the hospital's facilities terminated? Does this sequence of events violate due process?Could this process be extended to remove physicians whose patient mix and practice patterns are particularly unprofitable for the institution? Physicians who might admit a large number of indigent patients or whose professional conduct of evaluation and treatment resulted in slow patient turnover and lengthy hospitalizations could be denied access to the facilities as a purely commercial decision irrespective of the professional implications and effect upon patient care.

Management firms and hospitals have insisted upon the separation of these functions, and courts in some jurisdictions have held that medical staff bylaws address issues of medical competence and quality of care, and contractual arrangements speak to the compelling issue of financial viability. Since recent changes in reimbursement and compensation have placed many health care institutions in jeopardy, there exists a sympathetic climate, especially when these decisions are not viewed in the overall context of the quality and standard of medical care. Attorneys for hospitals and management companies agree that to involve the hospital's professional board would significantly undercut the institution's ability to respond to changing financial challenges and to make important business judgments. The administrator of the medical institution must assume the role of consensus maker in this regard.

The Supreme Court of Tennessee, in *Lewisburg Community Hospital v. David Alfredson, MD*, ruled that the medical staff bylaws constituted a binding contract between the health care institution and its physicians and that unilaterally voiding contracts and denying physician access to facilities sidesteps medical staff bylaws which require notice and a hearing before terminating hospital privileges. This decision formally links hospital privileges with hospital access. While this line of reasoning has not been universally accepted by all jurisdictions, there appears to be a strong public policy interest in maintaining significant professional oversight from the medical staff in decisions that affect the quality of patient care.

Exclusive medical contracts offer advantages to both provider and consumer in many instances. The interrelationships of financial and medical considerations are often complex and may work at cross purposes. Professional quality in our present environment will realistically be determined by considerations of availability, access, and financial viability. The medical administrator must develop a particular sensitivity for these issues in the next several decades. Balancing cost containment issues while maintaining standards and quality of care will continue to be an ever-increasing challenge.

Chapter 25

STANDARD OF CARE: CHANGES RELATED TO MEDICAL INNOVATION

With the development of specialty and subspecialty practices, ethical and professional decisions about what constitutes "standard of care" have passed from a local to a national jurisdiction and are being challenged by frequent changes in technology. Recently, development of expensive medical technology and regulation of distribution and access through health-policy changes in reimbursement and legislative initiatives have created further complexities in the development and maintenance of standards of care.

The profession of medicine, the legal profession, policy makers, and public representatives must reach agreement concerning the criteria used to judge the delivery of health care. The medical administrator must develop appropriate responses to present and future challenges in establishing such standards in an environment characterized by the rapid introduction of significant innovations, by escalating costs, by altered public perceptions and by finite resources. Standard of care is a basic tenet of medical practice and is employed by the legal profession and health policy makers to guide their conduct. The recasting and redefining of standard of care will be necessary to respond to societal demands and must relate to contemporary economic and social changes.

In recent years, health-care practitioners have had to respond to continuously escalating health-care costs, regulation by non-physicians of both access to and distribution of resources, improvements in technology, and a more informed and demanding public. Each of these phenomena has increased in number and complexity. In meeting these challenges, medical practitioners or health policy makers no longer can apply historic precedents or extrapolate from traditional medical practices to determine the appropriateness of a certain activity, policy, or regulation. Should "standard of care" be recast in light of changing technology, especially in an area as costly as medical imaging, specialization and subspecialization in medicine, regulatory intrusion, and changes in compensation methods?

Historically, the concept of "standard of care" was a legal one; presumably, it had its origins when persons engaged in health care sought to ensure quality by developing entry standards and a rigorous period of academic study, to be followed by organized training in the provision of care. From this arrangement, the professions and society came to accept a certain body of facts and a certain mode of activity as "standard" for the training and performance of a physician. Traditionally, the physician/patient relationship was the fundamental provider/consumer unit. In the last one-half century, this arrangement has been modified by the introduction of new technology and pharmaceuticals and has been greatly influenced by the growth of specialty and subspecialty training. Practice patterns have become more complex and advances in biomedical engineering have tended to separate physicians from the patients and, in like manner, have isolated the patient from the evaluation process regarding what constitutes standards of care.

The traditional legal concept of "standard of care" implied an analysis of local community standards. A physician was held liable only to that level of competence, concern, and compassion which society would expect of the average physician in the community in which he/she practiced. As more physicians entered various forms of specialized practice, the community standard became a national standard for each particular discipline. The local concept of "standard of care" was largely abandoned and to ensure a level of competence that would protect the public, the profession came to rely on specialty-board requirements and the certification procedure of the individual by that physician controlled credentialling body.

Traditionally, under a benevolent management, health-care facilities applied liberal criteria in deciding which physicians would receive staff appointments and privileges in their institutions. However, in the 1970s (as noted elsewhere), hospitals became much more aware of the legal implications of physician privileges and the need to have a rigorous methodology to assure quality assurance of practice by those physicians. Thereafter definitions of "standards of care," which until then had been controlled almost entirely by physicians, were modified by more broad-based entry requirements that explored previous personal conduct, physician performance contracts in more business-like terms, and the growth and influence of non-physician management in hospitals by administrators.

Concurrently there were unprecedented medical innovations. There has also been introduction of new policies and regulations, alteration of practice patterns and arrangements, and a growth of new disciplines. All of these developments had a particular impact on medical-imaging technology, which will be used as a paradigm in this discussion. However, these innovations have had profound effects upon the concept and importance of "standard of care" in all branches of medicine.

After Roentgen's discovery in 1895, innovations during the next five decades included the image intensifier in the 1950s and the scintillation camera and 99m-technetium in the 1960s. However, the introduction of x-ray computed tomography (CT) led to major changes in health-care policy which altered significantly the concept of "standard of care" for all of medicine. Legislation creating certificates of need, while intending to regulate the numbers and distribution of these instruments, also limited physician and patient access to them. While in the U.S. such regulation was administered at a local level, Canada and England through national policies attempted to match distribution with need and with available resources. Thus, in the U.S. the possession of CT technology soon became an important element in any determination of standard of care for certain medical activities and for the evaluation of certain disease processes. Although by the mid- to late-1970s CT became the standard in the evaluation of most central nervous system diseases, years passed before we had relative efficacy data for other anatomic areas (such as the chest) and systems (such as the musculoskeletal) to make these determinations. Often, the appropriateness of a particular patient's diagnostic evaluation was judged on the basis of anecdotal data only, since the results of well-conceived and meaningful studies were not available.

Following the advent of gray-scale ultrasound in 1973-74, these instruments, because they were relatively inexpensive and had no known significant biological hazard, achieved widespread use and distribution. Physicians from a broad range of training and experience began to acquire and use these machines in the absence of a credentialling body or criteria to ensure competence in the field of diagnostic sonography. Later in the decade, these machines became more expensive with the addition of real-time capability and pulsed Doppler and the procedures required more physician time for their performance. Soon, disputes arose regarding which specialty should control and operate these devices and who should determine standards of care.

In the 1980s, magnetic resonance imaging (MRI) was introduced into the clinical armamentarium. Although it proved to be more diagnostically efficacious in certain diseases, MRI was even more costly than CT. Subsequently, in the U.S., increasing health-care costs gave rise to greater regulation by such agencies as the Food and Drug Administration, the Health Care Financing Administration and the state agencies established to monitor the distribution of expensive technology and to issue certificates of need. Again, Canada and Great Britain developed a more global policy for the distribution of MRI facilities and their use.

Favorable tax laws to promote entrepreneurship and an increase in venture capital led to the development of a new type of facility - the medical imaging center that often was owned and controlled by non-physicians. This meant that now a scarce medical resource was controlled by a group with, at best, a different concept of standard of care and, at worst, little interest in the concept unless it promised to increase profitability.

At times, the various arrangements introduced to encourage the capital investment needed to acquire these devices circumvented the stated public policy to limit distribution while continuing to ensure patient access. In these imaging centers, the profit motive often became paramount and the selection of patients and the pressure to make profitable use of a major capital investment superseded medical standards or even clinical necessity.

In almost all areas except the central nervous system and spinal region, we have few if any reliable efficacy data concerning the value of MRI in various anatomical areas, systems or specific diseases. We seem to have accepted these procedures and gained assurance of reimbursement in a progression on the basis of body area (brain, spine...) and field strength (0.35 T, 0.5 T, 1.5 T...) for each manufacturer, rather than by demonstrating advances in knowledge concerning appropriate clinical application. In some measure, these technical developments changed the time-honored criteria for "standard of care" as applied to the alternatives in medical imaging such as comparison of ultrasound, CT and MRI.

Traditionally, the analysis of decisions about standards of care has been greatly assisted by the general acceptance of specific criteria. Thus, in the professional perspective, training and certification have been essential ingredients for these determinations. However, medical technology has created many levels of expertise and a variety of opportunities for the physician's involvement with these devices, which challenge traditional divisions of labor and service in health care.

In the U.S., despite numerous legal challenges by other disciplines seeking to gain control of these devices and the proliferation of medical imaging centers, society has assigned the ownership and use of CT and MRI largely to the discipline of radiology. Since other imaging technology such as nuclear medicine devices, conventional radiographic machines, and ultrasound was also owned and utilized by the radiologists, they should be less likely to duplicate and overuse equipment. Similarly, but on a much more limited basis, radiology was also allowed to acquire control of positron emission tomography (PET). To date, because its clinical use has been so limited, PET does not enter into considerations of standards of care but assuredly will in the future.

The concept of "standard of care" also has been altered by the introduction and subsequent improvements in gray-scale and real-time ultrasound, especially in obstetrics, where these procedures are now almost routine in standard prepartum care. Many obstetricians in private practice and in obstetrical and gynecological departments in hospitals and other provider institutions have their own ultrasound machines and interpret the studies they perform on their own patients. While standard of care before the introduction of real-time devices might have permitted the technologist to perform a study, which subsequently the physician would interpret, real-time studies, by the nature in which the data is accumulated, require the physician's direct participation to be performed correctly changing the practice and standard of care.

While these seem to be nuances, they are important ones and must be understood by the medical administration. Society is at the preliminary stages in the administration of education and certification of ultrasound services and many other technologically-based medical disciplines. As part of the professional's training experience, many specialty boards, e.g., radiology and obstetrics/ gynecology, require experience with the new technologies. Although the specialty's qualifying examinations require evidence of familiarity with the principles of ultrasound technology and interpretation, these bodies do not provide or require a standard test of competence. There is no special examination leading to certification in ultrasound. However, candidates can acquire a certificate and statement of "special competence in nuclear medicine" from the American Board of Radiology by completing an additional examination. Such procedures may have important implications for those physicians who obtain the approval of institutions and agencies to acquire and use these devices and to be compensated for such services. If such documents become mandatory, this process may assume practical importance in setting future standards because data will accumulate from this experience.

Concerning the process of certification and credentialling, specialty societies have made progress only to the level of policy recommendations and general suggestions concerning the training and experience needed to engage in these new technical procedures. The guidelines of the American Institute of Ultrasound in Medicine, for example, recommend "six months experience in performing and interpreting studies" as a minimum for the practice of real-time ultrasound. However, this guideline does not formulate a "standard of care" concerning the use of ultrasound in specific medical situations. However, with the absence of regularized criteria, it may be the most significant factor in determining "standard of care."

Recent changes such as technical innovations and reimbursement patterns often have substituted legal definitions of "standard of care" for ethical and sometimes commercial concepts. Physicians find technology interesting and intellectually rewarding, and ownership and control of these devices convey status and influence. Ownership and control of these devices may render clinical practice more efficient and convenient, and in a free enterprise system such investments may be financially rewarding.

Despite legislation to control the compensation of hospital-based physicians, it appears that regulatory bodies have given little thought to the effect that these and other cost-regulating initiatives may have on quality and standard care. Refusal of permission to acquire an MRI and CT device in the denial of a certificate of need (CON) will alter significantly the medical practice in the petitioning institution. This refusal also will limit the choices of the patients and referring physicians. The competent manager must be aware of these phenomona and allocate resources to appropriately respond to the imposed practice charges.

Often policy issues contaminate concepts of quality control: for example, regulatory agencies introduced relative value units (RVU's) to reward "cognitive" medical care or diagnosis-related groups (DRGs) in order to limit overall health-care expenditures. These measures have made hospitals less likely to invest in MRI and CT devices. While professionals provide most medical services in hospitals under exclusive contracts, either documented or implied, others who want access to these responsibilities or to a part of the service (such as brain scan interpretation) may mount a legal challenge to these arrangements.

Turf issues in medicine arise chiefly in relation to use of expensive equipment, interpretation of certain diagnositc studies within the context of a service (such as only those medical images of a particular organ system), or to the performance of certain highly compensated procedures. For example, groups of neurologists and neurosurgeons may ask to be certified as the official interpreter of central nervous system studies obtained on a CT or MRI device. Because there are not yet established firm guidelines that specify which specialties can own and use these instruments and because there are no presently recognized credentialling processes, it is almost impossible for the administration of an institution to determine a "standard". In some instances, in the hospital setting, departmental chairmen for the various specialties may take the responsibility for setting a "standard." Often these activities are self-serving and other disciplines may view them as a barrier to access and use rather than an attempt to effect proper quality control.

Medical groups, specialties, and societies may feel obligated to develop standards and credentials ostensibly to protect the public by ensuring quality; however, the public might view these efforts as a method of self preservation even though the setting of standards involves substantial risk, namely professional risks to the members and tort risks to the association. Those who set standards are expected to abide by them and to respond to questions about accountability based upon them.

Any standard of practice has the potential to restrain trade by acting as a barrier to access and use. An antitrust challenge asks not if the standard protects patient welfare but whether it promotes or suppresses competition; in this legal analysis, the motives of the professional society are important but are difficult to determine. The law will uphold standards imposed by societies if they measure performance and are not promulgated to exclude competitors. Discovery by legal depositions and documentary evidence of the society's purpose is important because the public can evaluate this characteristic - at least much better than they can evaluate the medical data that forms the basis for a particular standard. The latter data may be highly technical, whereas the purpose can be seen easily in human terms.

Once promulgated, standards may be accepted and applied rigidly by governing bodies and the courts. The landmark case of *Koefoot v. American College of Surgeons* (ACS) illustrates this point. The ACS took the position that if a surgeon performs an operation, then he/she should be present to administer follow-up care. Dr. Koefoot unsuccessfully challenged this decision because it required his presence and affected his practice patterns. He did so on the grounds that these requirements restricted competition and acted as a restraint of trade.

In the promulgation of standards, due process must be observed. The action, *Northwest Wholesale Stationers. Inc. v. Pacific Stationers*, established that the liability of any society setting standards was greatly increased by failure to provide due process. Any society, in promulgating standards, should provide due process and make a contemporaneous record of the procedure. The standard should be based upon sound economic and medical reasons rather than self interest and the intent to discriminate. Due process should ensure that physicians are given a reasonable opportunity to demonstrate their competence to perform a certain act or medical service. Medical administrators must have a working knowledge of due process. They are ultimately responsible if their institutional policies violate this concept.

In a technological discipline such as medicine, the application of performance standards of the instrumentation and standards in the appropriate use of this expensive and ever-changing technology have inherent risks. In the U.S. certain analogies in commercial law have set precedents for medical activities. In *American Society of Mechanical Engineers v. Hydrolevel Corporation*, a standard was set for a certain boiler part. An evaluation panel decided that the boiler part manufactured by the Hydrolevel Corporation did not meet the industry standard, thus virtually preventing its sale. However, an important fact was that a member of the evaluation panel was an employee of a competing manufacturer.

The Supreme Court found the Society of Mechanical Engineers liable for treble damages because it had allowed someone with a conflict of interest to influence the decision that victimized the Hydrolevel Corporation. Thus, self-serving and discriminatory standards can engender liability under antitrust considerations. Medical administrators, in assigning review boards, should be mindful of this principle.

The imposed standard itself may give rise to a new liability for any group which developed the standard. Standards can be interpreted to ensure a certain level of performance or to fix responsibility for safety of instrument function. For example, if the gantry of a CT scanner malfunctions, a surgical instrument stent breaks inside an anatomical lumen, or a monitoring device induces an anxiety attack, the physician and credentialling institution may be held to bear ultimate responsibility.

The existence of standards can and does increase the liability (to claims of malpractice) of those who promulgate these guidelines or certify practitioners, using those standards. Thus, the standards adopted by a medical institution should be reasonable and reflect prudent and ethical expectations for physician conduct. These may need modification with improvements in procedures and advances in technology. They should promote patient welfare but with a realistic appreciation of the resources available.

In summary, the consumer public expects the medical profession to develop standards which enhance patient care by ensuring quality. As medical circumstances change in response to technological development, new standards of care may be introduced or earlier standards may be redefined. To meet these changing responsibilities, medical authorities and specialty groups should develop new training programs and require a defined level of experience before certification and should gather data on efficacy.

Certification and credentialling bodies will need to develop appropriate examining, evaluating, and testing methods to ensure that health providers continue to develop and then to meet standards of care. Public authorities should recognize and address the consequences of competition between various specialty and subspecialty boards at the national and international level, rather than allowing local and regional decisions to set standards in an *ad hoc* and often self-serving fashion.

As standards are promulgated, those authorities who develop them should keep in mind that this process carries with it significant liabilities. Any privileges which accrue from certification are accompanied by attendant responsibilities and obligations. All parties concerned should expect such grave commitments in an endeavor as important as the delivery of medical care.

Chapter 26

SWIMMING WITH THE BARRACUDAS

The popular book *Swim with the Sharks Without Being Eaten Alive* supposedly contains singular information and tactical strategies that have proven of great value in business - or life, for that matter. It is written in a lively fashion and the situations are entertaining, but it speaks quite obliquely or not at all to the administrative environment in a large medical center. The analogy of the sharks is all wrong for medicine. Sharks are, to many, the true embodiment of evil; but, in general, their reputation has really been greatly embellished by a series of rather mindless movies, even the characterization in *The Old Man and the Sea*, and the failure of the general public to appreciate their true characteristics and limitations. Many sharks are fast but not quick and mobile, they possess only marginal eyesight, have little imagination and will only become aroused upon provocation. This characterization would not be appropriate for most of the players in the mix of complex medical centers: the administrator of the hospital, department chairmen, and one's own staff.

These groups will likely be fast and quick, bright and imaginative, possess extraordinary powers of sight and insight (no judgement intended for accuracy), have self-activating arousal characteristics, and feed long past satiation. These are not sharks (would that they were!); these are barracudas. So the book to write should be entitled *Swim with the Barracudas and Triumph*. Surviving is having too little space, a meager capital expenditure budget, minimal opportunity for advancement, and being viewed as a service-only group by the institution. The administrator and flock must do better than merely survive: they must triumph!

The barracuda is swift, has good eyesight (especially for shiny objects like US machines and CT and MRI scanners) and is tenacious. Therefore, you cannot avoid the creature, but you must develop administrative strategies to deal with the barracuda on an ongoing basis. Do not "chum" (to attract the barracuda) with your junior staff; rather, use them to gather data and assist in creating a consensus. When the moment of truth approaches, deal with barracudas yourself and one-on-one if possible so that you and the adversary have flexibility and are not encumbered by "posturing for the troops." If the issue is such that you believe it will be too sophisticated for your adversary, then bring along an expert witness posed as a "friend of the court;" but do not include a cheering section or the barracuda may choose to ignore the proffered expert and feed on the bait fish. Strength is in numbers of well presented facts not in how many people you have put in the water. Do not pack the arena with your friendly colleagues.

When you and your staff swim with the barracudas, you will survive on guile and spontaneity more than on the performance criteria that seem, to others, to be the natural outflow of the activity. To achieve efficiency at the expense of creativity is generally not what leadership needs in order to survive. Thinking in the daily routine of your key people is the most valuable aspect of their activity. They need to be spontaneous and creative, and you need to convey by encouragement and example that this is a very important lifestyle in your administrative unit. The barracudas will have greater difficulty with a moving target than with a stationary one and even greater difficulty when the movement pattern is unpredictable. As consultants, your constituency should not provide just the correct interpretation but also an innovative thought.

To survive with the "'cudas," you have to have a mix of managers and medical entrepreneurs in your stable. If all are the former you may succumb to boredom, and if all are entrepreneurs you may be crushed in the chaos. Entrepreneurs abhor what they perceive as bureaucracy but usually are able to communicate a sense of importance about their interests to the managers. This latter trait may make the managers' lives more interesting, but it increases the risks to the institution when the entrepreneurs are exercising their functions.

In fighting off the barracudas, remember not to be too flashy or the success equivalent of "shiny." This will make them feel obligated to strike. However, posing as accomplished and formidable without being superficial and shallow is adopting the right posture. That also does not mean that you have to be unduly modest. The happy medium lies somewhere between "the meek shall inherit the earth" and "it ain't bragging if you done it" (Will Rogers).

Survival in the midst of the barracudas does not mean that when you have achieved a great deal you should discard your ambition. Also, if you were accomplished enough to garner the wealth, kudos, or whatever, you are probably ambitious enough that these successes will not be permanently satisfying. You will return to the water and compete for additional resources. Just convince the barracudas that this is the natural order of things. Use a bit of egocentricity bias on them (a Madison Avenue psychological term for optimism).

Most administrators think that the technique of surviving with the barracudas was first articulated by the folk hero Satchel Page: "Run like hell because whatever's back there may be gaining on you." Not so! You have as much chance of running from a barracuda as you would from Carl Lewis - they are simply too fast and enjoy pursuing a fleeing prey. Become a General Jackson ("Stonewall") if you plan to stand and hold or "Old Hickory" if you plan to be more aggressive and are interested in a counter-offensive.

Barracudas have little or no memory. Just because you convinced them of the wisdom of a line of reasoning in the 1980s does not ensure success in the 1990s. If you proved the wisdom of an activity last year does not mean that you will not have to explain it from the ground up as an annual event — it could even be semi-annual. Do not become bored with repetition, revisiting a particular subject or covering ground in which your footprints are numerous and unmistakable. The barracudas will not, and failing to do so may stimulate them to strike.

Thus, swimming with the sharks is not to be compared with swimming with the barracudas. The stakes may be the same, but the adversary and the proper administrative tactics are not. Medical waters are filled with barracudas, and sharks are just bottom feeders in this environment.

Chapter 27

SURVIVAL MANAGEMENT IN A LITIGIOUS ENVIRONMENT

An almost unmentionable subject in administrative discussions is the effect of litigation. One of the most difficult tasks is managing a medical unit of any type during a lawsuit. The effect upon operations can be devastating, and morale among the staff becomes a significant problem. Physicians, individually and collectively, have unique problems with litigation. They have difficulties in levels of acceptance with the entire legal system. One reason is that the personal affront of the adversarial character of litigation is almost impossible for a physician to accept. To physicians, legal charges become personal attacks and, when made public, cause incredible anxiety. Among health care workers, this provokes a compelling urge for an immediate and victorious response when challenged; however, the legal system is structured not for this but for a series of sequential and seemingly unending deliberations, and the issue of winning or losing is moot. There are no "winners" in litigation, except for those in charge of the system, the lawyers.

A fact of life regarding medical malpractice suits is that they challenge the fundamental values that separate medicine from many other professions. Physicians are extremely proud (sometimes to a fault) of their medical knowledge and skills. This makes them both formidable and vulnerable in the litigation arena. Physicians wish passionately to be thought of as exercising the virtues of their knowledge and compassion for the benefit of those to whom they minister. Lawsuits usually claim that they did not exercise proper knowledge and skill, and may also imply that the physician did not measure up due to conduct that was willfull. Most physicians simply cannot handle this circumstance alone, and with good reason. They have been educated and practice in an environment which stresses the team approach and collegiality. Medical education and the practice of medicine emphasizes the advantages of compatibility, group effort, and cooperation. Traditionally physicians have had little preparation to accommodate litigation or have had little support from the discipline.

Another phenomenon that occurs within medical institutions when members have litigation visited upon them is that of distancing by other staff persons. Those members of the staff not named in the litigation often treat the defendants as if they had a fatal communicable disease. The isolation and lack of expected moral support and compassion for the accused can be overwhelming. "They treat me like I am guilty...as if I did those things the plaintiff's lawyer claims." Another fact of present society is that the suit may also be featured on page one of the local newspaper, ensuring the loss of any hope of privacy and confidentiality. After all, doctors make good press. Those who are accused also will come to know that if they are exonerated in court the account will be on page ten in small print. All news is not equal and, after all, doctors are supposed to do the right thing. What is newsworthy about the fact that this has been reaffirmed? The threat of paranoia among the staff and a divided camp must be addressed by proper management strategy. You must lead your staff to realistic expectations.

As Mark McCormick notes in his book **The Trouble with Lawyers**, the legal system works not to the advantage of the litigants or to the social system but for the benefit of the chess masters - the lawyers. The amount of staff time spent in interrogations, depositions, practical conferences, requests for dismissal and the trial itself requires a multiple of the time anticipated or allowed. In a medical service specialty, this can be an economic disaster and detrimental to patient welfare in the institution. For example, for what could represent an apparently frivolous suit alleging arachnoiditis following a myelogram, a neuroradiology team could be essentially unavailable for patient care for several weeks, responding to legal challenges designed to accomplish this situation. There are no Kelly Girl Services or SWAT teams to employ in this circumstance, so one may be forced to reduce the schedule or manage the logistics of transporting the patients to another facility to perform a necessary activity. Colleagues may or may not be understanding, but they will certainly not be pleased.

As the CEO, your accused staff will ask for your advice and counsel, although you may know less about legal procedure and risk of litigation than they do. By definition, you are in the leadership role, so you are expected to be "the point man in the minefield." When they become inpatient with the lawyers, you may receive part of the expression of their frustration. Lawyers base their careers on diverting hostility and using the anger of others for their benefit.

Another area that the administrator may be thrust into involves settlement. Physicians consider settlement an admission of guilt. In fact, this is a compromise that they believe threatens their professional career and even speaks to their personal honesty and motivation. The insurance carrier conversely is in a business, and settlement may be merely a method of limiting financial exposure.

For them, there is no moral issue involved, and they may attempt to enlist the administrative leader in arriving at this favorable economic arrangement. Staff will predictably have different criteria to judge the administrator's loyalty than will the insurance company or even the parent institution.

Malpractice litigation is a bit like bull riding: you would like to avoid it altogether, but if you understand the basics it may not seem so formidable. To manage this potential havoc, a candid discussion of the meaning of malpractice litigation will be helpful to your associates in managing the stress and minimizing the stigma associated with the complaint and possible media coverage. You can extend an invitation to both the best defense and plaintiff malpractice lawyers you can identify. Have them meet informally with your associates in a congenial setting. These guests can provide a bit of preventive nurturing if you direct them beforehand and are candid in your purpose. Given the opportunity, most lawyers will be reassuring to a potential client and stress the safeguards in the system and the protection afforded by their competence. We all have fears and even fantasies about litigation, and these informal sessions may prove to be the proper forum for the staff to work on theirs individually and collectively.

Our misconceptions about the legal profession are understandable if our data base consists of a distillation of "Perry Mason," "Night Court," and "L.A. Law" and newspaper accounts of the courtroom performances of Melvin Belli, F. Lee Bailey, Percy Foreman, or Jim Neal. Your staff will anticipate being rendered powerless by the legal system and that the entire process is designed for the triumph of the plaintiff. What they need to learn is that the legal system is, in general, a very cumbersome and all too expensive procedural methodology that usually arrives at a version of the truth. Albeit traumatic, the legal process serves as a method of dispute resolution. One should not engage in selfreproach and flagellation for having been ensnared in this unfamiliar process, but should instead devote one's energies to minimizing the defendant's pain and suffering. If there has, indeed, been malpractice, then a reasonable compensation to the plaintiff should be anticipated in monetary recognition of a mistake and not a criminal act.

The management of the collective behavior of the medical unit should be directed toward the support of the defendant's fellow staff members. The concept of these associates acting in a collegial and nurturing manner should be discussed by the CEO. Isolating the defendant by not expressing sympathy under the old saw "I didn't want to remind him because it might be upsetting" is simply a rationalization at best. This lawsuit will be on the mind of a highly motivated, proud physician from the moment of initiation to long after it has been completed. One cannot be "reminded" of something that is constantly on one's mind, and continued expressions of support are needed.

Ignoring the lawsuit actually serves as a method of assuring the other staff that they will remain untainted by this evil circumstance and makes the guilt feelings of the defendant much more real and forceful. At the same time that the defendant's lawyer (your collective advocate) is telling him that "this is the process; do not take these allegations personally," his colleagues are treating him as if he were a pariah. This makes the defendant's emotional accommodation difficult if not impossible. If this behavior is properly identified before a medical malpractice trial and the CEO has discussed with the staff how it will be viewed by the institutional conscience, then its effect should be much less devastating than having it go unrecognized or uninterpreted. Medical groups or departments can be polarized by this behavior, and the disappointment and, later, resentment can affect relationships long after the litigation is over. The feeling of being abandoned by one's colleagues lasts. If the defendant feels this abandonment was unfair and unfeeling, then the team concept is very difficult to reestablish.

There is a management role to the activity of settlement also. The first goal should be to have the defendant understand that victory in the courtroom is not a realistic expectation. The legal system is much too imperfect for that. Given this as an *a priori*, compromise may be seen as a victory of sorts. Because physicians so intensely believe in right and wrong, they need guidance in working through their interpretation of the fact that someone may need to be compensated when they did no wrong because the system affords this type of redress. Fundamental to one's entire medical career is the respect and good will of one's medical colleagues, and this is being threatened by the litigation process.

You should treat these physicians who are defendants in a lawsuit as if they were impaired, and provide the same type of support and compassion you would to a staff person suffering from alcoholism or substance abuse. These people feel just as powerless, if not more so; their problem may be publicly displayed in the local media, and there are no clearly defined or accepted safe havens. If and when they become depressed, they will now take on the stigma of mental illness to add to the embarrassment of the plaintiff's accusations. Compromise could be viewed by the defendant as an affirmation of all of these woes that have been visited upon him. You need to provide for whatever support is deemed necessary.

The present focus regarding medical malpractice is on prevention and risk management, and correctly so. Most institutions have awareness programs that identify areas and patterns of behavior that place physicians at greater risk. These should be supported and initiated by the administrative leadership. This is truly a case of "avoid the lawyers; they are hazardous to your physical and fiscal health." Not so well appreciated is the value of discussions of medical malpractice litigation, both from the mechanics and the emotional impact. Conflict resolution by compromise is also not addressed to the extent that it should be, nor is the collective institutional role during this stressful experience. Keeping one's course during a turbulent sea requires some prior thought about the challenges and responses in rough weather conditions. This is not defeatism; it is simply prudent management.

Chapter 28

AN ADMINISTRATIVE PITFALL: REWARDING NEGATIVE BEHAVIOR

The complexities of medical institutions are sufficiently great that administrators must be aware not only of the active and proactive aspects of their leadership but oftentimes the reaction for employee behavior they may encourage by their actions as well. One of the more insidious of these is a pattern of rewarding the activities and attitudes of staff that have a negative impact upon the progress and morale of the institution. In some regards, this is the alternative error in failing to reward those members who make significant contributions that have little public characteristics and easily go unrecognized and unnoted.

In a medical institution, levels of frustration often reach such heights that they have a variety of manifestations in staff behavior. The administrative leader should recognize this and manage the circumstance in such a way that the frustrations are acknowledged and dealt with so that the responsibilities are discharged, the staff member feels satisfied, and the other members of the department observe a positive outcome. For example, those faculty who handle frustration by public tirades, memoranda to clinicians containing provocations to invite an even more competitive circumstance, or circumventing the departmental administration to appeal to the institutional leadership should not be rewarded by a response to "fix that which is wrong" only. To do so will not only legitimize this detrimental style and pattern of behavior but will encourage other members of the institution to adopt similar techniques. Certainly, the management team must address the problem (or perceived problem) but in such a manner that the cooperative and caring image of the unit is maintained. The Hemingway ideal of "grace under adversity" should be encouraged.

The greatest dilemma occurs when a medical unit acknowledges that a problem exists but the administration of the institution is either unwilling to acknowledge that problem or unable or unwilling to commit the resources to solve it. In industry, if production of a product is compromised, sales will fall and profits diminish. In medicine, it is much more difficult to quantitate the impact of lack of appropriate instrumentation, technologists, and support personnel, so that the institutional administration may feel comfortable in not addressing a problem until a crisis occurs. This crisis style of administration may generate negative behavior in the staff because, short of resignation, this may be perceived as the most appropriate technique to get the attention of the institution.

It is not sufficient for the leadership to not react to negative modes of conduct; instead, it is essential that the institutional leadership generate an environment whereby frustrations are addressed in a timely fashion, commitments made with respect to technology and personnel, or reasonable explanations delivered as to why such commitments cannot be made at present - and when they will be made. This is the type of managerial leadership that is required to discourage negative behavior.

In dealing with physician demands, it may become mutually apparent that their desires cannot be met without additional resources from the institution. Then it is appropriate to inform the institutional administration of the need, but not because of the negative behavior manifest by your staff or the other physicians, but as a result of the legitimacy of the circumstance. Unquestionably, the allocation of resources in a medical department is an administrative challenge. The effort of any one staff member or other employee is difficult to quantitate more so than the number of procedures, or clinic days, or professional income derived from the individual effort.

One might take an entirely socialistic viewpoint and apportion the resources equally, providing no reward for either incentive or excellence. Alternatively, one might reward according to volume of production. This by-the-numbers approach can have some weighting factors, but in certain disciplines, specific activities may be highly compensated and others barely cover or fail to cover the overhead expense. In the near future, these patterns will largely be determined by third parties and may not be realistically in the control of the medical administration. Quite often in departments, the level of compensation is determined by individual faculty/administrative leadership interaction. Those staff members most vocal and insistent in their demands may receive a disproportionate share of the resources because the administration feels most threatened by them. This behavior, if it becomes a clearly recognized administrative pattern, is the ultimate reward for negative behavior. Over a period of time, it will encourage more and more of thestaff to engage in this "financial brinkmanship," creating a consistently volatile circumstance whereby the institutional mind-set is not that quality, contributions, and productivity are the criteria for reward but that demands and threats are.

Compensation issues are addressed in a much more healthy environment when the leadership meets with each individual staff member on an annual basis and discusses compensation in a global sense (not only salaries but fringe benefits and malpractice need to be reviewed in great detail, so that each staff member is knowledgeable about his entire compensation package.) Additionally, institutional leadership must consider the strategy used in professional sports whereby contracts are issued for multiple years. In the current environment, when staff have an annual contract, essentially all faculty members are free agents annually. If a staff member is told what their compensation package will be for the next year, the following year, and possibly the year after that, and if this is a comprehensive presentation, each staff can either sign on or indicate that they are going to seek employment elsewhere. If the individual signs on to the contract, this lessens anxiety concerning multiple, untimely, and unplanned resignations.

Besides not reacting to this brinkmanship type of behavior, the administration should practice a form of preventive medicine by informing staff what parameters will be used to determine the allocation of resources and the rationale for doing so. If these determinations seem to be acceptable, then these criteria should be adhered to. In most universities, there are guidelines for raises, and in the private sector, cost of living increases are a matter of public record. If the president (chancellor) and dean (vice chancellor) have set a limit of percent salary increase, the administrator will gain nothing by withholding that from the faculty, nor should they, in a moment of administrative panic, accede to the immediacy of the demands of an individual staff member to circumvent those guidelines for one and decrease the percent raise for a deserving but less vocal faculty member. "Robbing Peter to pay Paul" will soon be perceived as "robbing" to reward negative behavior.

In those academic institutions where the president or chancellor and dean or vice-chancellor have set a limit on percentage of salary increase, and where the faculty perceives this as unfair, it sometimes is helpful for the departmental chairman to review some universal compensation profile (in academics, the AAMC) with the leadership of the institutions. The leadership of the department must be seen by the staff or other members as the interface individual with the institutional leadership, and effective discussions with frequent reporting back to the medical department will help to decrease frustrations with compensation packages at levels that are perceived by the other members of the group to be inappropriate. If the faculty note that a certain service, or subservice, is receiving an inappropriate level of compensation, or if new members of the group are compensated at a higher level than loyal members of long-standing, morale suffers; ultimately, these talented individuals will seek opportunities elsewhere. Effective leadership requires effective communication upward to the leadership of the institution and downward to members of the department. It has to be communicated with clarity and precision that end-runs around the leadership of the department are intolerable, and that the departmental leadership philosophy will not be compromised because of inappropriate behavior by an individual or individuals. Stated another way, the leadership of the department has to indicate that in a team concept no person is indispensable, and that if an individual is sufficiently dissatisfied with the leadership and overall direction of the department, opportunities are better sought elsewhere.

In large medical departments, support personnel are often shared for reasons of efficiency and economics. Almost always, certain staff have difficulties with this sharing process. They often make such demands upon the support personnel that rather than assess this staff person's true needs, they will be rewarded for their negative behavior by acquiring additional support personnel just for them. In the short term, this appears to be a satisfactory solution: the support personnel feel less pressured, the rewarded staff are pleased over the outcome of this behavior, but the rest of the membership has observed yet another affirmation of the "squeaky wheel." A much more appropriate administrative response would have been to first inform the faculty person that their technique was not appropriate but that their need would be assessed by the administration and, if legitimate, attempts would be made to address these needs. The major difference may lie in behavior modification of the staff member.

It is absolutely a cornerstone of human resource management that individual behavior is extraordinarily difficult to modify. The leadership of the medical department may be able to indicate to a member of the group how their behavior is injurious not only to the department but to the member as well. The chairman can indicate that alternative strategies may have resulted in obtaining the goal with fewer repercussions for the individual, the department or the institution. However, to date, no medication has been found that instantaneously supplies maturity, judgment, responsibility and appropriateness.

Another expression of this leadership theory is that individuals do not change. Just as leopards do not alter their spots, those individual staff members whose behavior is sufficiently disruptive as to result in embarrassment for the chairman, embarrassment for the department, and embarrassment for the individual need to be guided to seek alternative opportunities elsewhere. Immature people do immature things that should have been addressed by their parents. If faculty members function in outlandish and disagreeable fashion, no amount of parenting by the leadership will correct behavior that should have been corrected decades previously. For the sake of the department and for the institution, these people need to be counselled, subsequently admonished, and then advised that such behavior if continued will result in termination.

Administrations must realize that the behavior of faculty and employees is certainly influenced by the circumstances of current life in the United States. Probably the area in which resource allocation has become most inappropriate is the field of professional sports, and the administrative leaders there have succumbed to the reward for negative behavior in the most improper fashion. One of the most highly compensated basketball players in the NBA does not even start for his team but comes off the bench. There are pitchers in both baseball leagues whose ERA should put them in the Hall of Infame but who will garner over a million dollars annually for their efforts in our national pastime. Players in the "skilled" positions in the NFL may be paid more than all of the offensive linemen, who perform the equivalent of routine physicals or possibly triage work. Some might say that this circumstance is a reaction to the days of yore when the administration had the bargaining power and the players were victims. Be that as it may, it was not these players who were involved. The present circumstance is largely a result of agent representation and an initial rewarding of negative behavior by several nervous owners.

The medical administration should adopt a posture somewhere between the legendary Vince Lombardi and the general administrative pattern that exists today. Lombardi dealt with his players directly. Upon learning that a future Hall of Fame lineman was to be in his office the next day with an agent to negotiate his anticipated salary, Lombardi felt this was negative behavior and detrimental to the morale of his team. When the player, who was a personal favorite of the coach and a great asset to the team, entered the office with his agent the next day, after exchanging pleasantries, Lombardi acknowledged their reason for being there but informed them that Green Bay was not the appropriate city. It seemed the player had been traded the previous afternoon to Philadelphia. I'm not suggesting that Lombardi was correct, but he did not reward what he perceived as negative behavior, and he demonstrated that he was willing to make a sacrifice to do so.

Certainly, there are times when the allocation of resources is not acceptable to every member of the department. One may find that the institutional administration will acquire an MRI and yet not hire as many file room personnel or technologists as are appropriate. As the administrator, one must acknowledge these inequities and indicate that, through rational negotiations and persuasion, these resource allocations will be brought into balance. However, to have an individual faculty member fire venomous memoranda or to directly make non-negotiable demands to the administrator is not appropriate and should not be rewarded. This will soon become a pattern and affect the image of your department and will undoubtedly compromise your institutional effectiveness.

Rewarding negative behavior is something that all administrators do, on occasion, in the interest of expediency or to momentarily still the roar of unrest. However, over time, this will not be in the best interests of the department or even for the person who engaged in the behavior in the first place.

Chapter 29

WHY DID I DO THAT ANYWAY?

One of the predictable facets of being a medical administrator is that decisions will have to be made and subsequently defended. In order to accomplish this, the manager will eventually have to define his motives, as well as his perceived mandate at the time of the decision or even the concurrent line of reasoning that was used. This circumstance can lead to occasional inner conflicts and, more importantly, a lack of understanding from and often the support of your constituency, especially the professional staff.

Most inexperienced administrators, in an effort to please and appease all of their various groups for which they have an obligatory advocacy, react to challenges and opportunities without a realistic consideration of what their true motives were. Sometimes, they fail to clearly identify which segment of their constituency it is that they are attempting to benefit by any particular decision. Later, when some type of accounting for their actions and decisions is requested, administrators, while feeling that they must have been entirely well motivated, have difficulty in explaining or justifying their actions. This failure of accountability comes not from a lack of laudable or appropriate motivation but from the absence of a "before the fact" formulation of personal policy and, retrospectively, a clearly articulated line of reasoning during the process. The tendency is not to recognize any single decision as a prudent one. Decisions create positions and these, taken together, represent policy if they reflect the actions, over time, of a senior administrator.

Why should a retrospective justification prove bothersome if one's intentions were ethical and moral, as well as just, and the execution of the decision fair and appropriate? There are several important reasons for this dichotomy. First, in medicine, we live in an environment demanding almost instant accountability. This is especially the fate of a service-oriented discipline, acting in a response role, utilizing high profile technology and delivering a vital product, health. Second, our circumstance is a very complex one in which there may exist equally valid demands for scarce and finite resources, and there may also be equally meritorious lines of reasoning leading to any decision among the alternatives. Given this circumstance, what is the administrator's accounting responsibility to the parent institution, to their staff, and to themselves? Must the administrator feel obligated to articulate the significant determinants of his reasoning process and to justify "why I did that"?

If managers are where they should be, at the summit of responsibility or the pinnacle of administrative leadership, what guidelines for their decisions should be employed? In truth, one can only be true to the collective conscience as the advocate for the institution. While institutional guidelines of conduct and responsibilities are important, these must be accommodated by the resources at the command of the individual managers as well as the character and orientation of the institution. For example, if an area has been designed and staffed to be service responsive, any erosion of this orientation should be resisted. If the administrator fails to do so, he may find himself reacting to a momentary perturbation inconsistent with long-term goals and not understood by his constituents. Space and technology for this service will have to be justified and the choices and alternatives explained just as resources for alternative activities are. Details and ventures into micromanagement should be minimized, as they will often limit future activity and are difficult to have all of those affected properly understand. When members of the staff make the microdecisions, the administrator is often not held accountable for the details.

There can be a flexible component to this accountability, but it requires a body of experience. The administrator should feel comfortable with making decisions by following their own inclinations and impressions, rather than seeking a consensus on every issue. Gradually, through the selection of staff, allocation of resources and space, and emphasis of certain programs, the institution will evolve in a direction that provides not only a clearly identifiable character but also a continuity that gives its endeavors a meaningful theme. Over the course of time, this is invaluable for continued success and will markedly decrease the need to explain, negotiate, and justify in detail the majority of one's activities.

Medicine is an exciting, technical, and serious discipline, and those characteristics should be embodied in the identification and image of the leadership as well as the staff. The CEO must not limit the scope of endeavors engaged in by the staff and should, in fact, encourage commitment in areas that are outside the historical traditions of the discipline. This should be done both for personal satisfaction and replenishment of the emotional energy needed for sustained inventiveness among staff members. The feeling of creativity and service to others make satisfied and successful staff. In these areas the staff should be encouraged to "do it for themselves" and find pleasure, giving a feeling of behavioral flexibility for both the administration and the staff. Nor should these activities have to be justified, as long as productivity and professionalism are maintained and each person's routine service areas are "covered".

This line of reasoning can be extrapolated into the professional life of an institution. The staff members are the most critical analysts and, in the end, they are the audience that the administrator would most like to have agree with their policies and activities. The administrator's role should be to have staff come to the realization and gain the confidence of knowing that their own opinion of their efforts is valid and very important. The staff should feel it is appropriate to please themselves and should feel it proper to declare "I thought it was correct at the time, the right thing to do and I would gain satisfaction from doing it." The CEO should reinforce this feeling and make every effort to assure the staff that they are being supported.

How is this accommodated with the administrator's usual role of advocate for the staff? Very well, since administrators can only excel at things they believe in. If the constituent group believes in an endeavor and they know the reasons for their conviction, the advocate's role becomes much easier. The administrator can have this latitude if he permits it in his faculty, and both will feel more creative.

Chapter 30

ADMINISTRATION: AN APPROPRIATE TRAINING SUBJECT?

Medicine today faces challenges that are unprecedented, and traditional administrative techniques to address these issues often seem to provide imperfect and partial solutions. Many leading periodicals and magazines for the general public have featured the various crises in medicine. Among the often cited major problems are the cost and distribution of, as well as access to, medical resources. Equally noted is the increase in malpractice litigation and the extended liability of physicians and medical institutions through agency relationships. Also mentioned are exclusive contracts and "turf" problems leading to issues of antitrust that are considered in this text. The complex relationships of health care employees, because of infrastructure and agency arrangements that characterize modern medicine as it is currently practiced in the United States, also provide challenges that require unprecedented management skills to address.

Traditional administrative techniques to address these issues do not provide solutions, and frustration abounds; consequently, professional turnover in management positions is high. Administrative leaders in all areas of medicine have almost always attained their status through achievement in other areas and have had almost no formal training and often little experience in the basics of management. In fact, one would specifically note that studies in administrative techniques and management are not a part of the usual medical school curriculum. Most medical schools have severe limitations of curriculum time, and new courses have limited success in acquiring entry into the didactic experience unless they increase traditional scientific knowledge. Ethics has been one area in which new exposure to a fundamental, but not necessarily fact-driven, discipline has been granted some limited access. Medical administration is an even less well identified subject, and while one might accept the intellectual argument of its importance, the granting of time in the already overloaded medical school curriculum has been problematical. Additionally, this subject is occasionally addressed in the specialty training period if at all.

Employees in certain areas of medicine are in very short supply. The shortage of general support personnel is so widespread that it is almost universal. Unions, collective bargaining, and litigation are a part of the reality of life as a medical administrator, due to changes in the attitudes of employees throughout the health care system. Compensation schemes have not only favored the expeditious turnaround of patients but have contained procedural emphasis as well, encouraging physician competition as to which group will perform the more highly compensated activities. The projected scheme of reimbursement (RBRVS) proposal by the Hsaio Report was predicted to ameliorate this stimulus for turf wars, but physicians will develop strategies to resist many of these changes, and the desire and competition for instrumentation to perform diagnostic and therapeutic procedures will continue. Managed care will predictably foster competition and also heighten tensions in the future.

The conflict in many instances is not just for technical resources but the infrastructure, including the control of support personnel, patient referral base, and the necessary space within the institutional environment. These challenges require a multifactorial learning process. Trainees, for example, should be taught the importance of specific education leading to their present or future credentialling process and how to present these effectively to the administration of an institution.

Technology holds intellectual fascination as well as prestige and control for the purveyor, which gives rise to conflict regarding possession and use of these resources between departments and their respective staffs. Doctor/doctor conflict resolution is an anathema to most physician leaders, because it is not only a problem for which they have had almost no training in the techniques that should be employed but is an issue they believe they should never have to address. Various societal and economic changes have made competition between specialties and even within disciplines a reality. Trainees should be made aware that this is an expected circumstance and that an appropriate response from them requires specific effort.

Are these management subjects only to be approached by independent study? Will the innate genius of physicians overcome any lack of technical knowledge and experience? Might we address this in the curriculum of our training programs? I believe that we must teach management techniques addressing these issues to our trainees. The following are some suggestions how we might proceed.

The most challenging issue for the medical administrator is that of conflict resolution. Conventional wisdom describes the practice of medicine to be relatively conflict-free, emanating from the fiduciary relationship of physicians and their patients, the traditional collegiality among doctors, and the learned professions' exemption from certain legal considerations such as antitrust. Also, we have historically been blessed with favorable reimbursement schedules that were largely determined by physicians, and the lack of such practices as collective bargaining or arbitration by employees.

The reality of today, however, is that conflicts between the physician and the patient are common. Conflict resolution between the many disparate parties in the health care system is probably the greatest challenge that the administration has to face.

Often, staff in departments and, more commonly, trainees do not appreciate fully the institutional considerations that are determinative in the process of resource allocation. They are unaware of the specifics of financial analysis that is a necessary part of a reasoned decision process. Trainees and junior staff become somewhat cognizant of these activities during budget negotiations, but a formal disclosure of the consideration during the process might be very instructive for the trainees and even therapeutic for the department leader and business manager. This does not need to be a disclosure of the specifics, but a general discussion of the various considerations would represent an improvement over what information sharing is presently available.

Later, without this exposure, when these same individuals find themselves thrust in positions of administrative leadership, these unfamiliar responsibilities may seem so overwhelming and anxiety-producing. A well-prepared justification for an institutional commitment is of great assistance in securing any particular acquisition. These *pro formas*, while complicated in the health care field, do not necessarily deviate greatly from common business practices, and an alternative to seminars on this subject taught by the chair or the departmental administrator could well be an educational experience conducted by a faculty member of the school of business administration or management. This latter method has been successfully incorporated in ethics and legal medicine courses of some medical schools and should be used as a role model.

The present compensation schemes favor abbreviated hospitalization, often causing a recurrent time warp between the capacities of the institution and the wishes of the clinicians and the perceived needs of their patients. Physicians often feel uncomfortable about the trade-off between the economic considerations and their compelling need to ensure the welfare of their patient. The realities of global reimbursement schemes and the specific demands upon the traditional physician/patient relationships and scheduling challenges often seem overwhelming.

While these responsibilities have a factual basis, they can also be addressed by management and administrative techniques. The usual circumstance found in present departments is that regulations are being promulgated at such a pace that the minimal or almost non-existent administrative techniques that have been historically employed are not appropriate. The most common mistake of the administrator is in not accurately assessing the problem, defining the necessary infrastructure to address the challenge and then preparing an appropriate request to the institution.

Certain well-established management strategies from business offer improved opportunities for success in health care. These can be taught as general principles and made to address more specific issues and challenges that arise in the conduct of the service responsibilities of medicine. Physicians have long proposed the theory that medicine is much too complex to be conducted as a business. This posture is no longer tenable, and it is now accepted that certain commercial aspects of medicine can only be effectively approached using sound business principles.

Just as lawyers hold moot court, physicians might benefit greatly from exercises in contract negotiation. Exclusive contracts represent the standard institutional relationships for certain medical disciplines, and contract law is a well-recognized subspecialty of the legal profession. The basics of this discipline could be presented and explained by having a hospital attorney substitute for the clinical conference approximately twice a year. Alternatively, most medical schools have a course in legal medicine, and arrangements could be made to have trainees attend the sessions on the law of contracts. Knowledge of the practical aspects of contracts, antitrust, and several other related legal subsets is essential in administering any medical unit.

Due to the rapidly changing patterns of reimbursement, knowledge of financial operations in medicine has become increasingly important. It is imperative that graduates be knowledgeable in CPT coding of procedures, ICD-9 coding of disease processes, and the philosophy underlying these regulations. In addition, knowledge of contractual arrangements based on HMOs and PPOs and fixed reimbursements based on the Relative Value Scale (RVS) are important in order to understand and evaluate reimbursement patterns - present and future. It is only through an understanding of the complexities of these topics that fee schedules which optimize reimbursement can be established and responded to appropriately.

Almost all hospitals now have a marketing department. The faculty person responsible for resident and fellow training, with some effort, should prepare a staff individual from marketing to give several sessions on issues and techniques specifically addressing the marketing challenges of a discipline such as medicine.

Our environment in medicine has become sufficiently complex that administrative skills must be a part of every successful physician's resources and facility. The techniques and methodology of administration are not part of the traditional medical training experience, but I believe that they should be. The challenge is to define those areas representing an appropriate course of training that will ensure some acceptable level of competence and to identify the proper context in which management training should occur. Resources in the department (chiefly the chairperson and the financial manager) represent the "first line" faculty. Hospital attorneys and administrators should also participate in a structured curriculum. In a university setting, seminars from appropriately chosen faculty members in disciplines of law, business, and policy can be effectively utilized. These sessions must occur within the time frame of the other traditional teaching sessions of the department in order to symbolize their "legitimacy." Certainly, the need for effective administration of our medical resources is a major current problem and will only increase in importance in the future.

Chapter 31

THE PERILS OF ADMINISTRATIVE BOREDOM

Among the many perils that befall the unwary manager is the insidious one of boredom. Often the onset of this malady is so gradual that it escapes the members of the staff and is totally unrecognized by the affected administrator. The signs and symptoms are very subtle and will exist for long periods of time without detection.

While administrative boredom is difficult to detect, awareness of the characteristic symptoms may facilitate the process. The specificity of symptoms will obviously depend upon many variables, including the administrator's environment. Boredom will often express itself in the administrator becoming aloof, withdrawn, and available to only a fraction of the staff. Rather than have the global interests necessary to administrate a complex biomedical enterprise, the chief administrator will choose to be very selective in his interests. Often, this will be an area in the discipline that has narrow clinical and academic bases. Faculty often derisively speak of these as "pet projects," and reaction to them ranges from reluctant acceptance to resentment.

Not only will the administrator be selectively reclusive but will manifest resistance to change or innovation. Time-honored management strategies will be continued without any current analysis of their present validity. Creative and aggressive staff often find this circumstance maddening. The staff will usually view the bored administrator as rigid, unimaginative, and uncaring. To overcome this perceived and real (though selfimposed) isolation, the administrator may turn to diversions which provide intellectual stimulation and satisfaction but are not relevant to the mission of the organization. This may work to repair the psyche of the bored administrator but can be detrimental to his image as a leader in the discipline. Diversions are emotionally replenishing but, if not kept in perspective, will compromise administrative success. They also send a mixed message to the other institutional leaders and those being led. Thus, each of these symptoms has a good likelihood of resulting in a significant institutional malady.

Once the diagnosis of administrative boredom has been made, is there appropriate treatment to effect a cure or at least to ameliorate the consequences? Boredom can be relieved by change, which can be either internal or external. The administrator may as well benefit from the change invoked by rearrangement of lines of responsibility. Rearrangement may also alter the administrative channels by which the medical unit interacts with the institution.

Oftentimes, change is perceived as inherently "good" by both internal and external respondents. Internally, those changes evoked should be associated with the concept of opportunity. Externally, the hospital and medical school administration may see this as a challenge. Reacting to such forces usually brings out creativity and enthusiasm. Not only will the change transport the administrator out of the boredom, but the external reinforcement will create momentum for the department.

Obviously, the value of this communication could be enhanced greatly if a general prescription for administrative boredom could be provided. Unfortunately, this cannot be done with any precision, because it is so dependent upon the environment in which the boredom occurred. Among the several specific possibilities is the transformation from a division-oriented department to one based upon subspecialty sections. This not only changes the players but the administrative relationships as well. Alternatively, possibilities for change might include the formation of a center or development of a research division or a foundation. Another may be the creation of a new service area such as an outpatient facility. Whether these suggestions will cure administrative boredom in every circumstance is impossible to predict, but such an outcome seems consistent with the character of the illness itself.

Chapter 32

DIVERSION: THE ADMINISTRATOR'S SALVATION

The complex, geometric growth in medicine ensures that the professional time of the administrator will be characterized by constant change, challenges of turf, financial concerns, and incompatible personnel interactions. The emotional energy that must be devoted to these challenges should be balanced or replenished by other activities that can fall under the general category of "diversions."

The term diversion connotes a departure, and therein lies a significant problem for the administrator. A fundamental precept of the work ethic is that all activities should in some way relate directly to one's profession or at the very least be useful and productive. The medical profession has been particularly constrained by this expectation, for the prototype physician was one who was always available and whose time was entirely at the disposal of the diseased and suffering. Most of us entered the health care field with this stereotype as our role model. Later, if for some compelling reason we wished to assume another posture or to move into areas of interest that were not directly related to this calling, questions of appropriateness were raised. Public expectations of health care providers have, indeed, influenced their historical choices.

Physicians involved in patient care can potentially exercise some control over their professional time by selecting the type and number of patients they will see and at what times these medical experiences will occur. Conversely, the administrator has much less control, as human interactions tend to be more complex, multiple, and in circumstances in which a manager has less of a fiduciary capacity. In dealing with colleagues it becomes exceedingly difficult not to be almost always available. Each staff member will feel their request for attention and time is of high priority and will almost never think in global or departmental terms. They would have to consider their time allocation multiplied by the total staff in the department that should have equal access to the administrator. Operating in this situation, many administrators reason that the demands upon their finite time are infinite. They then gradually begin to allocate more and more of their day (and night) to activities related to their profession. They are certainly encouraged to do this by both their supervisors and their employees.

After a number of years of this insidious change, the administrator will come to realize that all they do is directly or indirectly administrate and that their professional life is their life. By this time, also, they may have reached the height of their discipline and their only counterparts on this lofty mountaintop are in other institutions at considerable geographic distance. Their former cohort group may now well be their employees — greatly changing the tenor of their personal relationships.

An administrator simply cannot depend upon occasional interactions with their alter ego at a national meeting nor expect those professional relationships flowing from the work situation to provide gratification that will be fulfilling on a long term basis. This is a compelling reason for and justification of a diversion. In a basic sense, it can be considered the preventive medicine for "flame out."

Choosing one's diversion need not have the intense quality of many professional decisions. A diversion for one administrator might be drudgery for another. Obviously, each person must decide both what provides pleasure and what represents sufficient change to add variety and replenish one's emotional drive and, hopefully, creativity. This can be arrived at by thoughtful analysis of interests or by unstructured trial and error in attempting available alternatives. As long as the activity is relatively healthy, wholesome, and honest, it is "acceptable." The natural diversion for a sedentary administrator would seem to be some type of physical activity. There are a variety of positive implications from exercise, but if running or walking seem like tedious "putting one foot in front of another," then the administrator might opt for a technique sport such as golf, tennis, or skiing if they can do it on a regular basis. They must try to steel themselves against rising at dawn to hit against a ball machine or to be the first on the practice tee. Unless the administrator is a "competition addict," they should not set a goal to win the state 45's singles or the first flight at the country club. There is great danger that the desire to excel at the diversion may make it an extension of their professional activity and provide no relief. A diversion must be enjoyable and probably not quantifiable to provide the intended benefit.

Physical diversions are not for every medical CEO. Anything that provides an opportunity to balance the stress of one's professional activities should be considered. If the nature of one's administrative activities is people-intense, a private intellectual pursuit might be preferred. Many successful administrators lose themselves in the scholarly adventure of becoming expert and being active in some form of collecting. Among the more popular for people in medicine are collecting paintings (1), antique furniture (2), oriental rugs (3), silver, and medical books and instruments. If the physical diversion is to hunt or fish, the administrator might also wish to consider collecting antique waterfowl decoys or handmade lures of yesteryear.

Another benefit to collecting as a diversion is that one is placed in a circumstance wherein their professional position is relatively immaterial, and they are judged and accepted on their expertise in the field and the type of person they are as a collector rather than the investiture of their professional position. While this could be viewed as a levelling experience, it relieves one of the need to posture and divests one of the responsibility to maintain a particular type of image or presence. Appropriate garb for a goose calling contest or gear for fly fishing for tarpon will easily conceal one's lofty mantle as director of the X, Y, or Z "Institute for Medical Progress." Even more important is that it simply does not matter.

Self esteem is important for the personalities that gain responsible positions in medical administrative leadership. A part of the ambition to achieve these highly visible and often stressful positions is often founded in the need for acclaim. As one proceeds further and further upwards in one's professional endeavors toward some ultimate and increasingly ill-defined goal, there are fewer and fewer people, on a personal basis, to appropriately understand and praise the accomplishments. Aspirations and personal accomplishments often become so complex that administrators sometimes lose their former support system. Colleagues tend to be intimidated by the nature of the manager's successes and no longer should be expected to provide the specific type of praise that they did formerly. An understanding of this phenomenon can lessen the feeling of loss that many administrators have, but appealing to a different audience through a satisfying diversion activity provides an even more viable alternative.

The pleasure of being recognized as an expert or even thought to be one in some form of diversion is a great boost to an administrator's self concept. When the administrator has started in the field of the diversion from ground level zero, it is a great pleasure to be recognized by another peer group. Again, one must discipline themselves against being enamored with the competitive aspects or going from one activity to another constantly seeking acclaim. If the administrator feels compelled to set goals or impose standards upon their diversion, they should make them modest ones and, when they have been achieved, savor these small accomplishments before pressing onward to the next. Smell the patina, bask in the 100 feet flycast, or the 250 yard drive (in the fairway).

Behavior modification is an often-lauded technique whereby the compulsive, sometimes obsessive, hyperactive overachiever executive/administrator can change to ensure emotional survival. Personal style and one's manner of conduct are exceedingly difficult to modify, although it may well be in the administrator's best interests. After all, this fundamental type behavior may be felt by the administrator and his colleagues to be the reason for their success. We tend to act upon intuitive patterns etched early in our development. To act and react in a different manner requires a significant rearrangement of values, which in itself is stressful. A partial solution, or at least a more pleasurable alternative, can be found in a well chosen diversion. Also, one can practice and experience a different type of behavioral pattern in an environment that is not crucial to one's success or cluttered with the expectations of others.

If you are the type of administrator who immediately addresses himself to a perceived problem, you will be predictably given more and more challenges to act upon. If in your diversion you can learn to be more patient (try clay court tennis or a Sotheby's art auction), even engage in "benign neglect," you will find that many "problems" posed to you never become a reality and those that do can be addressed in a more studied manner. Patience can become an acquired virtue.

The issue of professional colleague acceptance and institutional understanding of the diversion activity arose earlier in this discussion and is a reality. Whether it can be achieved varies with the traditional attitudes held in the environment in which one works and in the expectation of others who are affected by the diversion. Negotiating an understanding based upon benefits to your personal welfare will have little appeal to your colleagues. Assuming that there will be no value judgments or criticism of your diversion is, at best, unrealistic and can be fatal. Sometimes, administrators attempt to avoid these unpleasant possibilities by concealing them. For example, one of America's foremost art dealers wrestled professionally for years under an assumed name; a department chair at a medical center steeped in the "work ethic" tradition entered local tennis tournaments by using a variation of his name that escaped identity to all but those in attendance at matches. These techniques eventually became self-defeating. Honesty and candor, while initially more difficult, will eventually create the circumstance wherein one (and the institution) will eventually reach an accommodation and the administrator will receive the greatest benefit from the diversion.

The phenomenon of "burn-out" has been highly publicized in the corporate world and more recently the medical profession. It is a significant problem, but one that has received less attention has been the loss of creativity after someone has occupied the same or a similar medical administrative role for a number of years. This is a greater problem because it erodes the success of a working unit or even an institution in such a gradual manner that it may go unrecognized for a very long period of time. It involves such a great number of people that this phenomenon, though unrecognized, has developed an inherent energy and philosophy. One can only remain creative if one has the emotional energy to do so. It is that energy which can be replenished by developing and engaging in a suitable diversion of one's energy once the true professional responsibilities have been discharged.

Chapter 33

BEWARE OF THE TRAPPINGS: CEOITIS

The current popular literature is replete with revelations of CEO administrative styles and inappropriate conduct that have led to the dismissal of innumerable giants of American industry. Certainly, parallels exist in the administration of hospitals and medical departments. Some management techniques apply to almost any type of endeavor, and those that are unsuccessful in one field may well apply to others. Among the most common causes of terminal CEOitis is the temptation of leaders to isolate themselves by insulating their administrations with the trappings of office and the tendency to surround themselves with "yes" persons and sycophants.

Trappings of office differ greatly with the industry one is evaluating. Several were described in the April 1991 cover story of *Business Week*. F. Ross Johnson's palatial hanger in Atlanta for RJR Nabisco's 26 corporate pilots and ten aircraft, complete with an elaborate waiting area which is now for sale for an asking price of only $10 million. An even more personal trapping was ascribed to Robert A. Schoellhorn of Abbott Laboratories who used Abbott monies to acquire two personal jets - the second presumably for his second wife, who had been his secretary. Only a few years later, when yet a more expensive "corporate" aircraft became available, $20 million of Abbott money purchased it.

Trappings become impediments to communication because they represent symbols of insensitivity. While certain prerogatives are due any CEO, these should not be of such magnitude that they serve to differentiate greatly from senior management, nor should they be resented by others in the organization who are responsibly fulfilling the requirements of their positions.

In a professional organization, the differential in benefits should be small by business standards and should reflect seniority, productivity, and responsibility in some acceptable fashion. In medical institutions, the CEO's salary may be a reflection of the standards of the industry related to the salary of specialties at other institutions. Since this is a quite democratic process and subject to very little manipulation by the CEO, the staff should be made aware of the mechanism by which this compensation is calculated.

The CEO should also have the same vacation and meeting days as the staff in a group practice. Meetings and practice-related absences should also be related in a responsible manner to the opportunities of others in the institution. This latter safeguard speaks to the issue of separateness and isolation. Certainly, trappings, benefits, and direct compensation represent symbols by which opinions by employees regarding the fairness are built. In American industry, the CEO's compensation is 85 times what the blue collar worker in that same industry makes, while in Japan the ratio more nearly approaches 10 to 1. Even the latter disparity would not be acceptable in a corporation of highly educated professionals.

There are certain characteristics and realities of positions having little to do with the hubris of the CEO that almost conspire to isolate and place him "out of touch" with the operation. If not accounted for by management strategy and personal style, these can cause CEoitis to be fatal. Information, once readily available to him as a young partner or middle management executive, becomes filtered by employees and faculty whose best interest is to curry favor and not so much to espouse the truth.

It was said of Frank Lorenzo that his reputation as a tough and ruthless CEO so intimidated his senior executives that they became unwilling to share data with him that could be viewed as negative and would appear to embrace and support his decisions, even though they might be well aware that they were not in the best interests of the Texas Air Corporation. In this circumstance, the corporation, a medical partnership may then be administrated under the inner agenda of the CEO fed upon by faulty or certainly biased data. A CEO's inner agenda is often centered upon the inner needs for self-esteem and fulfillment as well as desires for control over people and activities in the business. Harold Geneen, whose autocratic style of leading ITT Corporation was legendary, had this bit of insight into CEO narcissism: "The worst disease affecting senior executives in the United States is not alcoholism, as popularly believed, but egotism. This impairs more CEOs than their martinis."

The behavior resulting from this egotism can lead to loss of morale in the organization despite the fact that the same inner drive was a motivating force for the CEO and previously for the employees. This apparent contradiction reflects the different outcomes or the difference in perceived results as they relate to the CEO. The success of the organization may not be graciously or fairly shared by the CEO; corporate triumphs, rather than enjoyed by the rank and file, are resented and may even sew seeds of jealousy if associated with prominent symbols of success enjoyed only by the CEO. Professional and civic honors as well as public and scientific kudos garnered by CEOs in their self-perceived role as "statesperson" may be viewed as excessive personal reward by the leader by what was in fact due to corporate effort. This is one area stressed heavily as a pitfall in the standard but unwritten manual of appropriate CEO behavior in Japanese industry.

In an ever-changing field such as medicine, CEOs must not only avoid CEoitis and immunize themselves against it, they should also have a well-defined administrative plan for CEO obsolescence. Our business parallels suggest that many CEOs ensure their longevity by surrounding themselves with individuals who have neither the ability nor desire to replace the CEO. The CEOs often have a history of eliminating the bright and forceful staff member who might eventually take their position. While this may provide a rather perverse form of job security and will certainly water the flower of narcissism, it also deprives the partnership of middle and upper management leadership. Eventually, it may well be the culture to grow the serum to cure CEoitis by removal of the offending alien - the narcissistic CEO. Instead, the CEO in a highly technical and rapidly advancing field such as medicine must either retain competency in one of its facets or develop an entirely separate set of skills that will sustain their needs to contribute in another related or unrelated field of endeavor. The $T_{1/2}$ of a CEO in medicine is short and sometimes mercifully so. Any prudent administration should have a management strategy to address this reality. Those who do not may fall prey to the more insidious malady of chronic CEO disease, which is less obvious than the acute form but often has the same outcome. CEOs become obsolete just as do the latest marvels of medical technology you have just acquired.

Chapter 34

THE MANAGEMENT OF CHANGE: AN ANTIDOTE TO ADMINISTRATIVE OBSOLESCENCE

Much has been written regarding the management of change and various administrative ploys to address the issue of responding to the variations and ever alternating differences in our professional environment. A related but less well recognized challenge that should be an integral part of any administrator's long-range management strategy - the creation of change in one's milieu and the development and alteration of one's administrative style as these occur to avoid the appearance of disinterest and obsolescence.

Most CEOs in medicine spend the initial few years of their career in a mode of building their institutions or departments by a series of continued acquisitions of resources related to space and personnel, which usually have the character of an institutional investment. They must function in a constant advocacy role in which the personal rewards are derived from recognition of the quite tangible resource acquisitions. The management style is often a very aggressive one and is encouraged by others who benefit, including one's colleagues because the administrator may well have been recruited to do precisely that. The sky is perceived as very blue, the sun is shining, and the progress is so visible that it borders upon being palpable. The probable and the possible may almost coexist, and practically everyone is caught up in the enthusiasm of obvious and tangible accomplishments. One's mandate may be so global that the constraints are almost not identifiable - Valhalla and Utopia are the CEO's next door neighbors. It is almost never a question of whether, but of how much and how many; creativity leading to growth and expansion will be applauded by the institutional conscience.

Difficult as it may be, CEOs must, at this time, develop a strategy to change their inner rewards and administrative style to reflect a future slowing if not a cessation of this exponential growth and to provide evidence for others which demonstrates the responsible and conscientious use of those resources acquired in the phase of rapid expansion. The "empire" by now may have been built; however, it must be managed in such a way as to demonstrate an appreciation for that which has been given and recognition that a more selective series of requests for institutional resources will be forthcoming in the future. Appreciation should not only be expressed verbally but also by one's actions.

A business analogy to this administrative scenario might well be the entrepreneurial phenomenon of a "start up" company that is now a reality and is to be brought to the "big board." After the initial investors have evaluated the management results (probably for the first time), they may or may not decide to go public with the present administration. During this period, the company's founders often have a tendency to treat the enterprise as their personal stepchild and thus have to force themselves to develop a more corporate management style. Failure to do this has resulted in the inability of many small companies to progress to the next level of growth. Expulsion of the leadership has often resulted because, for the first time, the investors have now become part of the active administration.

The nature of a service-based and visibly expensive discipline such as medical imaging, for example, lends itself readily to the concept of "investment" by the institution and often an awareness by the clinical specialties of the magnitude of the resource allocation. This recognized commitment of resources has with it the tacit reciprocal or expectation that a return on investment should occur. A prudent CEO of this administrative unit should plan, after the sustained growth period, to change their management style to address this evolution in perceived responsibility. To remain "appropriate," this CEO must administrate in response to the natural change that has occurred.

The perception of management obsolescence can take a number of forms and be symbolically expressed in all manner of ways. In the aftermath of technological prosperity and professional achievement, the pall of boredom and apathy can enter the collective staff consciousness because the CEO has not anticipated or planned for an appropriate administrative change. This proposed management strategy does not necessarily mean that one should administer toward zero growth or program for lack of progress, but the CEO should anticipate a posture which may well represent a redirection of energies and a change in resource requirements. Those activities that require visible and tangible institution resources may need to be substituted by more programmatic endeavors. For example, the CEO might plan for an expansion of the wellness center or, in an academic institution, CME instead of yet another capital expenditure or construction of a diagnostic or treatment facility, unless these are perceived as being absolutely necessary for the welfare of the institution. Administrative energy could be directed to the improvement of public relations at the "front desk," information transfer, or the career ladder for the support personnel.

This means also that the personal needs of CEOs for satisfaction in their professional activities may need to be redirected internally. The successes in these more primary functional areas will predictably not receive the public acclaim of former achievements nor will they have the equivalent symbolic implications in the areas of influence and control. In a sense, the CEO will not only need to develop different management strategies to effect this change but must anticipate different rewards and receive satisfaction - often from a different locus. Not to redirect some energy to the more programmatic areas will invite administrative obsolescence as well as boredom and loss of direction and enthusiasm for one's position. Adding other types of resources will be recognized by one's colleagues and the public but often carries with it considerable risk if it is not perceived as appropriate and needed by the institutional conscience.

The realities in service-based areas may, indeed, preclude the administration of change in certain areas. When CEOs become convinced that they are unable to change their circumstances in a particular area such as technology acquisition due to external or internal constraints that are real, then they may need to redirect their energies and either change their interests or choose another venue. A considered and rational decision not to remain as the CEO or the same type of CEO is an honorable one. There is life after any particular type of administrative leadership, and personal fulfillment does not always mean being "at the point." Inner needs can be satisfied by private accomplishments or the reflected accomplishments of one's colleagues.

While the thesis of this communication has largely dealt with the response to anticipated change as a methodology to foster continued success and enthusiasm for one's position as administrative leader, one must recognize that change in the context of this discussion is not always possible. One should be certain, however, that this lack of opportunity was not due to a failure to manage the change but may well be because of circumstances beyond one's purview. The certainties in life include death, taxes, and, most certainly, change.

Chapter 35

DISCIPLINE: AN ESSENTIAL QUALITY FOR ADMINISTRATIVE SUCCESS

If one examines the biographies and autobiographies of successful people throughout the centuries, one particular characteristic stands out above all others, and that is personal discipline. Even those aberrant personalities and seemingly unconventional lifestyles of certain great leaders have this undercurrent thread of discipline. Found among those who may not have been appreciated for their greatness until late in their careers or at all during their lifetimes is also this element of discipline, "stick-toitiveness, bullheadedness, or dogged determination."

Discipline does not have the creative attractiveness of the ubiquitous term charisma, the modern catch phrase of pizzazz, or the special gift associated with genius, but it outshines all of these as an administrative quality that will consistently result in personal and leadership success. Discipline does not have to mean predictable, nor does it have to connote dull or be equated with boring. It can certainly lead to creative success and instill confidence in the group that you have chosen to lead. There must be a DNA code for discipline (yet undiscovered), a text on how to teach it and instill it in others (yet unpublished), or a universal role model (yet uncovered) which await these future events. This chapter will explore the value of this concept in the context of current analysis and contemporary references.

In researching the history of the Civil War, the two central figures (wearing opposite colors) and ultimate protagonists were Robert E. Lee and Ulysses S. Grant. First, to dispel the myth of "conventional wisdom," U.S. Grant was not a bumbling alcoholic but an outstanding tactician and a fierce military leader. Here were two successful men from incredibly different backgrounds who manifested totally different management styles but were contemporaneously successful.

Robert E. Lee, the ultimate patrician, impeccably attired, tall, erect, astride his white horse, was the descendent of such legendary figures as Light Horse Harry and Richard Lightfoot Lee. An honors graduate of the U.S. Military Academy, he had declined the leadership of the Union forces extended by

President Abraham Lincoln to remain loyal to his native state of Virginia. He was such an effective leader that many of his victories, especially the first Battle of Bull Run (Manassas), were against substantial odds. With all of his distractions, trappings, and myriad interests, Robert E. Lee had the personal dignity of discipline that was recognized by his followers at every level and inspired them to often be "better than they were."

In almost total contrast was the taciturn, rather inarticulate, physically unimposing, and, for a large part of his career, undistinguished Ulysses S. Grant. Prior to the capture of Vicksburg to gain control of the Mississippi River for the Union forces, Grant had a quite minor command of a small body of the Kentucky regiment. Vicksburg, located high on a bluff above a bend in the Mississippi River, had proven to be impenetrable from the north for both superior numbers of troops and some of the best military minds of the Union forces. Grant devised a scheme to float southward under the Confederate guns and attack from the south. Under the rationale of speed, but I believe to instill discipline and resolve, Grant ordered his men to take so few supplies that, if they were not successful in capturing this naturally fortified city, they would for a very long time go hungry. Recognizing the futility of his position when he discovered Grant's deception, the Confederate general in charge of Vicksburg sent a communique to Grant asking what were the most favorable terms of capitulation acceptable, whereupon Grant replied "unconditional surrender," hence another interpretation of the "U.S." of this most disciplined leader.

At Appomattox, Lee, elegantly clad in a newly pressed uniform, surrendered to a smaller man dressed in a borrowed private's jacket upon which the general's epaulets had been temporarily secured. Both were successful leaders because they had the common ingredient of personal discipline. Lee had won most of the encounters and inspired his troops, and Grant pursued his mission with great resolve and sheer doggedness. Once, following Vicksburg, Grant had sustained such heavy losses to achieve a dubious military goal that Congress, to voice their disapproval, asked President Lincoln to relieve Grant of command. The President showed his faith in the unpopular general with the reply "I can't fire Grant; he fights." I suspect that this thought was a part of the logic of the men who fought under "Unconditional Surrender" Grant.

"Stonewall" Jackson was not always Stonewall. He certainly was not a grand success in life early on and enjoyed few advantages that came to him unearned. An orphan with only rudimentary educational opportunities and preparation, he somehow secured an appointment to West Point. His educational background was so deficient that his first two years on the Hudson were quite problematic, and he was given little chance of graduating. However, Jackson finished in the upper third of the class, and the commandant remarked "had the course been five years, he would have graduated with honors." His military career was so underdistinguished that he soon found himself in a teaching post at Virginia Military Institute. There, his strict discipline, teaching oratory, fundamental religious fervor, and his inability to adjust to academic life rendered him unpopular and largely unsuccessful in that environment. Yet it was this same resolve and discipline which made him an extraordinary leader of men whose style "by example" was so effective that when his left arm was amputated due to a battle wound, Lee remarked "he has lost his left arm, but I have lost my right arm." The better-known quote about this disciplined American, however, was "observe Jackson's line holding like a stone wall." After his death some eight days following his injury, his command was henceforth known as the Stonewall Brigade.

In Fuzzy Thurston's novel about the Green Bay Packers under the almost-mythical figure, Vince Lombardi, players would take the field and perform while injured, as a demonstration to their coach of their dedication and discipline. John Unitas and Raymond Berry probably never had the innate physical skills of many players in the National Football League, but most fans believe that they invented the two-minute drill. The two-minute offense requires maximum discipline under maximum pressure. Thomas Alva Edison, when asked about his genius as the necessary ingredient of his personal success, is said to have attributed his accomplishments to about 5% inspiration and 95% perspiration. Perspiration, we believe, referred not to sweat but to persistence and discipline.

Most researchers will tell you how easy it is to fashion research protocols and at times gather the appropriate data. They lament the fact that after this is all done, waiting for the inspiration to initiate the manuscript is often so very difficult. Those that conquer this hurdle get asked "How do you write so much?" Implied in this query is that these scholars have uncovered some technique about which much of the writing effort is somehow obviated. Candidly and honestly, the answer is simply "one word at a time." What is not stated and often goes unappreciated is that this requires a self-imposed discipline which may not be a natural tendency for most people.

Few Americans will ever forget the lone figure of the Watergate proceedings who steadfastly refused to reveal what he knew. He was variously characterized as a scoundrel, deranged, and misguided, and, largely for the interpretation of his uncooperative posture, received a stiff penalty at a time when his co-conspirators freely passed their responsibility to others by statements such as: "The President made me do it. I had no idea about a plan. I was deceived. My role was insignificant. It was just part of my job. I knew it was illegal, but the Attorney General approved. Washington is a fickle place, and those who do not cooperate are soon on the streets seeking reemployment."

There was a solitary figure who adopted a contrasting posture in all of that nadir of national credibility, and he said: "We had an important mission, and I was told and believed that it was essential to the national security of my country. My orders, as far as I know, came from the Oval Office and I executed those orders. I believe what we did was in the best interest of my country, and I am proud to have been a part of this overall effort. Furthermore, I believed it to be in the interest of national security, and I am neither going to reveal certain facts in a public forum nor am I going to apologize for doing something that was in America's best interest. If I must be incarcerated for the maximum sentence, so be it." It will be difficult to forget the image of G. Gordon Liddy emerging from the hearings walking erect, proud, and at the "point" with his legal representation following behind.

A decade later, I found myself on a flight sitting next to a small, impeccably attired man who was also quite absorbed in his writing. We had ordered the same diet mutually assumed that it would be agreeable to "waste" about 10 minutes engaging in light conversation. He told me that he was putting together a speech for an address at a university. Against my better judgment, I asked him "Are you Gordon Liddy?" His reply was a very simple, straightforward response, "I am," and we both finished our meal and returned to our writing.

Upon departing the plane in Washington (how fitting!), I was again struck by the fact and that I was half a head taller and about 50 pounds heavier than this man, whose public personae had evolved from a misguided zealot to the ultimate soldier. I immediately went to the airport book shop and purchased **Will**, which is a lifelong saga of discipline and how to acquire it and to use it. Several years later, as part of an annual campus event at my university, the highlight was a debate between Timothy Leary and G. Gordon Liddy on the virtues of doing what feels good versus doing was is good and bearing the pain and ridicule through discipline. Liddy received a standing ovation.

When working in the Starling Physiology Laboratory at University College under Hugh Davson in the mid-1970s, I was impressed at the discipline of this very famous and accomplished man. Davson would briefly "visit" in the morning with each researcher in the laboratory and then retire to his office and write until "ll-sies," edit his morning's work, and repair to one of the local pubs for "lunch." Upon return, he would enquire how the experiments were progressing and then retire again to write. At about midafternoon, he would emerge for one final consultation, depart the laboratory with a briefcase filled with manuscripts, footnotes, articles copied by his secretary, and some product of Emily Bronte's (his favorite writer) and catch his train down South to Wimbledon.

From observing this, I gained two very important insights: that my former concept of discipline in writing had been totally naive, and that discipline was more important to writing success than an honors course in English.

There is an old adage that if, as the administrator, you have a task that is important and difficult, assign it to the person who already has the most difficult and important responsibilities, in order to maximize the opportunity for success. This speaks more to the quality and effectiveness of discipline than to respect for sheer ability of one individual versus another. The earth is populated by starters and finishers; finishers are disciplined individuals. Although there are inherently steadfast characteristics of discipline in most activities of medicine, to administrate something as complex and sophisticated as medicine requires discipline to task.

Each day, you will receive a new Medicare ruling; the latest demands from Union 101 to respond to; a notice that the lease payment for MRI #3 is overdue from financial management; of the 600 applicants for your six residency positions, you have one who is the direct descendent of Sir William Osler but finished last in the class at the Medical College of Belize; if you will be on the Board of Founders of a new venture, "X-Rays Are Us," something truly wonderful will happen to you; or perhaps the agent for your staff opening (the same agent that represented "Hotrod" Williams and Dwight Gooden) is calling for an appointment to renegotiate his contract in light of another offer. Discipline will allow you to assign priorities, apply the due diligence (a great term learned in business school) necessary for an informed analysis, and to exercise these administrative responsibilities promptly and with due care. If they seem overwhelming in the conglomerate, discipline yourself to set priorities by your value (not pleasure) system, request data and advice (not so you will have group therapy or a committee to share the responsibility should the decision be unpopular, but because you need it), and never procrastinate in hopes that the challenge will disappear, unless you believe it will. Discipline yourself as an administrator never to grease a well-oiled, smooth running machine just to reaffirm your continued participation.

Discipline yourself never to "steal the thunder" of the achievement of an employee. This appears to be a very difficult task for medical administrators, as I have discussed previously. Your discipline in this regard will be rewarded manyfold, not only by the continued achievement of that particular employee but by the realization of others that they will not inappropriately be required to share their success. There are many well-known administrators whose employee T 1/2 is notoriously short - a sort of "great place to be from but I wouldn't want to live there." Thus, among the eleven (or so) commandments of the good book of administrative success, just behind compassion and fairness is discipline. When completely surrounded by the Indians, Custer failed to exercise the discipline necessary to formulate a military plan. However, disciplined analysis allowed Creighton Abrams, upon being informed that the German tanks and soldiers had encircled his army, to conclude, "the poor________, we have them just where we want them," meaning of course that he could break through their perimeter in any direction he chose, and he knew his resolve would allow him to do so.

Discipline will not only get you there but may allow you to understand how you did it and more importantly will instill the confidence in you among those you administrate.

Chapter 36

ETHICS IN CURRENT MEDICINE

The complexities of modern health care delivery have restructured the relationships of providers and recipients of the service as well as the interrelationships among providers themselves. These differences in our historical modes of the initiation and response provide unprecedented challenges regarding judgments of what constitutes ethical behavior. To manage, these complexities should be recast in the context of our historical traditions. In this chapter I hope to offer some observations regarding the effects of our present environment, and suggest analysis and attitudes that appear to have future administrative promise.

Traditionally, medicine involved almost exclusively the fundamental relationship of patient and physician — the physician with an all-encompassing fiduciary capacity and the patient in a dependent and accepting role. Most of the principles embodied in the Hippocratic Oath and other guidelines of practice conduct reflected this private and quite personal arrangement. Ethical behavior in medicine has traditionally evolved over a rather lengthy period of time; these codes of ethical conduct were primarily based upon personal human relationships and an ordered morality (with a primary aegis in religious fundamentals) and was relatively uncluttered by concurrent economic considerations or by initiatives from other professions. Ethical canons in medicine by mid-century came to occupy an intermediate temporal position in their evolution as advances in science entered the practice, ushering in a more rapid phase of discovery and innovation.

The legal system continued to develop its own behavioral guidelines in its rather ponderous method of litigation and decisions leading to the establishment of precedents and legislation to formulate laws and influence public policy. This deliberate and almost leisurely pace enjoyed by the medical profession in the development of ethics was also characterized by self analysis, self determination, and self regulation. Those few changes in professional behavior that occurred among physicians went largely unchallenged, either by other practitioners of the discipline or by the consumers of their services.

While medical ministry was indeed a service, patients viewed the physician as someone to be admired who had undergone considerable personal sacrifice in order to be competent to perform this service and to be allowed to practice what is considered a valued calling. Correctly or not, the advantaged position of the medical profession was accepted as a natural consequence of the rigorous requirements of entry and the importance of the activity to society. In general, there were only a small number of recognized professions, and these were regarded with considerable respect by those whom they served.

Until the mid-20th century, medicine was also characterized by its lack of definitive methodologies to diagnose and treat human diseases. Much of the care extended to patients by the staff was in the form of nurture and providing physical comfort, with little application of complicated and expensive diagnostic technology and treatment methods. The process of healing depended largely upon the powers of the human body and spirit. The physician's role was in guiding the patients and families through this process. The medical staff was a recognized part of the cure, but the physician was not equated with or considered the cure itself.

In the decades after mid-century, the character of medicine has changed dramatically. Scientific discoveries and technical innovations were applied to the diagnosis and treatment of disease. Medical technologies were developed that required large sums of public resources. In response to the practice opportunities, physicians began to specialize and subspecialize, entering into areas of practice that were quite different and unique. This changed both the personal conduct of medical staff and their relations with patients and fellow physicians as well. Confidence in relief and cure for disease shifted from the fundamental nurturing unit of the personal physician/patient relationship to the more impersonal one with the physician acting as purveyor of this new and powerful modalities.

Trust and hope on the part of the consumer-patient became confidence and expectation. The physician often became remote from the patient and little, if any, personal relationship was established. Managing medical enterprises became a great challenge in public relations. Initially, the newness of this phenomenon resulted in an enthusiasm and almost awe that was accorded the pioneers in its development and the early users who employed this technology. Public programs were developed to foster health care institutions such as hospitals that provided the appropriate locations for these advances, and methodologies of compensation were enacted to support their growth. Medical management became increasingly important.

Following the Second World War, the groundswell of national pride made Americans confident that our industry, energy, and spirit would make all things possible in the decades to follow. Many technical advances developed during the War could be and were applied to medicine. The delivery of health care moved from what was, at most, a small, personal cottage industry to a major business enterprise involving and consuming a significant portion of public resources. Those persons entrusted with formulating health policy began to regard this in an entirely new light. Physician behavior in this enterprise became one of a participant in an only partially understood growth phenomenon over which they had much less influence and control than in their historical relationships.

Medical administrators were often the designated advocates in procuring these medical resources and, as such, had few guidelines as to what represented proper behavior. Understandably, as patients and their physicians became aware of these advances, the desire for access was the determinant of their actions. As restraints were utilized by policy makers to limit and regulate the distribution of these resources, physicians entered into various financial arrangements where the unstated intent was to circumvent these regulations. These entrepreneurial schemes involved physicians and medical institutions in ownership of the resources that they employ on patients for whom they have control. Often, their co-investors are businessmen whose primary, if not sole, agenda is to make a profit. The ethics of these arrangements sometimes becomes a consideration of legality and not of what constitutes proper professional conduct. It may be as the Chairman of Chrysler has opined, "When money talks, theology walks."

Another initiative to regulate the use of certain medical resources has been the inaction of diagnostic related groups (DRGs). This methodology allows only a certain amount of financial resources to be utilized in the evaluation and treatment of a particular constellation of symptoms and presumed diagnoses. Many health policy analysts felt that DRGs were a prospective pricing system that would determine the type of medical practice physicians could be compensated for rendering.

In order to circumvent this form of regulation, physicians soon learned those presumptive diagnoses that would allow them the most financial latitude in their evaluation and treatment. Physicians were encouraged by hospitals to discharge patients before the allowable funds were exceeded, as the hospital would be forced to assume responsibility for "overruns." Patients might be discharged and almost immediately readmittted to then be considered under a new diagnostic scheme and with renewed potential funding.

Physicians soon found themselves in the role of "gatekeeper," distributing care according to guidelines set by others, rather than practicing without constraint all the medicine they felt necessary in order to diagnose and treat their patients. Managing this change became problematic. Physicians and administrators felt frustrated because they were unable to meet the expectations of patients regarding the use of these resources. This frustration was sometimes manifest by circumventing the DRG guidelines under the rationale that the physicians knew what was best for their patients and the activities of those physicians and medical administrators are an expression of this mandate.

More recently, Congress and the Department of Health and Human Services have embarked upon programs to restructure the practice of medicine, employing guidelines of practice that would essentially regulate physician activities. The effects of these guidelines upon medical administration may be profound. It is believed that we have entered into an era in which the technological and procedural practice of medicine is too highly compensated and the "cognitive" (hands-on) practice of medicine is undercompensated. Therefore, a reformed system of compensation has been proposed to address this issue. A group of economists and policy makers with the consultation of physicians have developed a resource-based relative value scale (RBRVS) to compensate physicians for their activities. Primary care involving patient and physician interaction are supposed to be more highly compensated, and technological procedures will become less.

Under the RBRVS system, physicians will now evaluate their intended course of action with a much greater weight placed upon their personal income. This economic decision is one in which physicians feel increasingly uncomfortable, and their behavior will often reflect an attempt to abrogate this responsibility that they believe has been thrust upon them. These changes will provide unprecedented challenges in medical administration.

In the last several decades, technology resources have come to be an important, if not the leading, factor in determination of the facility and image of a health care institution. The most highly regarded hospitals have the most sophisticated computed tomographic (CT) scanner, the latest magneticresonance imaging (MRI) devices, the newest angiographic laboratories, color pulsed Doppler ultrasound machines, and possibly a cyclotron/positron emission tomography (PET) facility. This technology may cost millions of dollars and has to be amortized by financial methodologies emphasizing their almost constant use in order to be profitable. Guidelines and regulations that provide economic disincentives to discontinue these practices have been characterized as a significant threat to the financial welfare of medical institutions in which the ownership of these facilities resides. Patients often choose to be cared for in these institutions because the technology exists there, and physicians seek privileges there because of the access they have to this technology. Medical administrators must acquire these resources and then properly manage them if they are to be successful.

The present administration must choose between the "fixing" of prices and compensation or managed care whereby bargaining and competition will reduce the cost of health care. The manager of medical resources must be a participant but not the advocate of the patient, the medical staff or the societal mandate.

Physicians are now at a junction in the evolution of health care where they are being challenged in their fiduciary capacity and are subject to an ever increasing accountability. Practice outcomes are now being judged in response to patient values and quantified whenever possible in public perceptions. Medical ethics are now acquiring a closer fit to human ethics in general and not to specialized standards historically accorded to the healing arts. Physicians and health care workers should make every effort to be an active and effective part of this process. The administrator must take a leadership role and factor those various initiatives in their management strategy.

Chapter 37

In Conclusion:

MOTHER'S LESSON FOR MEDICAL ADMINISTRATION

The complexity of American medicine, and life in America for that matter, has made oracles of those who have been recognized as being successful administrators. When these persons attempt to explain and characterize their success, they all seem to get very complicated in their analysis and convoluted in their explanations. Some seem to justify this success by casting it in terms of survival in an extremely difficult environment, while other administrators conjure up a cerebral style that others try to emulate because it seems to eliminate conflict.

Most successful administrators get trapped into the lengthy and convoluted justifications and even rationalizations of their achievement because they believe such an explanation is expected. Administrative success is based upon fundamental human principles and basic responses, and style, systems, and methods have been vastly overrated.

We like to think that physicians are unique people blessed with superior intellect, incredible discipline, and a genuine desire to benefit humanity. Our detractors might suggest that our brilliant minds are narrow in focus, the discipline an expression of wanton ambition, and a large part of the benefit from our services relegated to self aggrandizement. More recently, physicians often have been characterized as arrogant and impatient individuals, possessed of large (if frail) egos, and fiercely independent. Taking this group collectively, medical administrators can identify their constituency. How then should someone plan to lead the flock?

Since most physicians are interested in being supported rather than driven by those in charge, you must adopt your mother's style of leading by encouragement. Your mother didn't engage in child abuse, so you shouldn't adopt an abusive style with your constituency. Sometimes when one of the employees commits an act that I consider a breach of professional etiquette, I do not visit the responsibility upon the employee but think "his mother should be spanked." I remember once that my director of Continuing Medical Education came to me during a symposium and was mortified that one of the invited guests had indicated that the honorarium (which the other speakers considered acceptable) was not what he felt was adequate. I told my staff physician that the other fellow's mama had probably told him he was special just once too often. This demanding physician is world famous in his subspecialty and is making substantial contributions to our discipline but has never achieved a major administrative post — he apparently did not have the appropriate MBA, mother's best advice.

Mother should have let you play with the others in the sandbox because if she had, you would have acquired several important administrative techniques there, like trading. You simply cannot have the bucket, the shovel, and the ball. In fact, in the proverbial sandbox,you not only learn to trade but *what* to trade; don't end up with the bucket and the ball, or the shovel and the ball, and if you can have only one thing — take the ball. Mother should also have sent you to the sandbox with something to trade. A successful administrator would never enter a negotiation without a bargaining tool or "chip". Mother is not responsible for teaching you what the other party wants to trade: you have to learn something on your own, but not anything important — just the nuances.

The successful administrator will compensate his employees fairly, but their remuneretion may not be seen as such. Sometimes one of your staff will come in during the salary discussions and tell you that you will have to increase his compensation because:

1) They just purchased a new Mercedes (Lexus, etc.).

2) Their child's summer camp will be $5,000 a month payable up front in yen (try the YMCA).

3) Tuition at their daughter's prep school will be doubled next year, not including violin lessons or the dental fee for braces.

Now, you can be offended by this behavior; after all, how could an adult with a dozen years of education come up with such reasoning? But, think of how pleased your mother was when you presented her with an infantile problem and an unreasonable demand. Because of her nurturing impulses she responded with understanding and compassion. Act like your mother would: have compassion and understanding, but do not even try to meet all the demands.

Several times a year some faculty member will exercise what they believe to be the "free agent" status. They will recount to you an offer they have had by another institution or group. The monetary compensation and fringe benefits will predictably exceed yours by 20 to 2000%. Given this circumstance, you have several choices as an administrator:

1) Panic and meet the offer, creating great inequities in your own group.

2) Become enraged and offended at this attempt at bribery (did someone mention extortion?).

3) Reflect upon the shortcomings of their mother and the virtues of yours. Their mother probably told them from 18 months onward that they were the smartest, best, etc.; but she forgot to tell them that she was biased and that there were other mothers out there drilling their little boys and girls with the same phrases. Your mother may have told you not to reveal this to others but to let them discover this on their own. In fact, your mother, by example, would never become visibly upset with your unreasonable demands; rather, she would be flattered that you wanted and expected so much of her. While being kind and not disputing your right to have delusions of grandeur, she would simply not let you have all that you wanted. She had the good judgement, however, not to let you feel refused, rejected, and unappreciated. As a successful administrator, you should know how to do this with equal facility.

In this complex world, we can only successfully administrate if we can simplify the challenges to the point where the solution can then be defined. The lessons taught by your mother were simple, and they were obviously effective and correct — just look at how well you turned out!

BIBLIOGRAPHY

Abraham KS. Medical liability reform: a conceptual framework. *Journal of the American Medical Association* 260:68-72, 1988.

Alpert G, McCarthy TR. Beyond Goldfarb: applying traditional antitrust analysis to changing health markets. *Antitrust Bulletin* 29:165-204, 1984.

Arnold WW, Pias J. *The Human Touch.* New York: John Wiley, 1993.

Asch SM, Lowe CU. The consensus development program: theory, process, and critique. *Knowledge: Creation, Diffusion, Utilization* 5:369-385,1984.

Barker JA. *Paradigms.* New York: William Morrow and Company, 1992.

Barnard CI. *The Functions of the Executive.* Cambridge, MA: Harvard University Press, 1968.

Beer M, Spector B, Lawrence PR, Mills DQ, Walton RE. *Managing Human Assets.* New York: Free Press, 1984.

Bennis W. *An Invented Life.* Reading, MA: Addison-Wesley Park, 1993.

Berry TH. *Managing the Total Quality Transformation.* New York: McGraw-Hill, 1991.

Bloom A. *The Closing of the American Mind.* New York: Simon & Schuster, 1987.

Brennan TA. Practice guidelines and malpractice litigation: collision or cohesion? *Journal of Health Politics, Policy and Law* 16:67-85, 1991.

Burns DD. *Feeling Good.* New York: William Morrow and Company, 1981.

Byham WC. *Shogun Management.* New York: Harper Collins, 1993.

Byrne JA, Symonds WC, Siler JF. CEO disease. *Business Week,* April 1, 1991.

Calvani T, James AE Jr. Antitrust law and the practice of medicine. *Journal of Legal Medicine* 1(4):75-102, 1980.

Casalino LP. Balancing incentives: how should physicians be reimbursed? *Journal of the American Medical Association* 267:403-405, 1992.

Chassin MR. Standards of care in medicine. *Inquiry* 25:437-453,1988.

Coastal Neuro-Psychiatric Associates PA. et al v. Onslow Memorial Hospital, Inc., 795 F2d 340 (4th Cir. 1986).

Cohen AR. *Portable MBA in Management.* New York: John Wiley and Sons, 1993.

Cohen H. *You Can Negotiate Anything.* New York: Harper, 1988.

Conner DR. *Managing at the Speed of Change.* New York: Villard Books, 1993.

Coulam C, Erickson JJ, Rollo FD, James AE Jr (eds). *The Physical Basis of Medical Imaging.* New York: Appleton-Century-Crofts, 1981.

Covey SR. *The Habits of Highly Effective People.* New York: Simon & Schuster, 1990.

Darling v. Charleston Community Memorial Hospital, 33 Ill. 2d 326, 211 N.E. 2d 253 (1965), cert. denied, 383 U.S. 946 (1966).

Deming WE. *Out of the Crisis.* Cambridge: Massachusetts Institute of Technology, 1992.

Drucker P. *Managing for the Future.* New York: Penguin Books, 1992.

Ellwood PM. The Shattuck Lecture. Outcomes management: a technology of patient experience. *New England Journal of Medicine* 318:1549-1556, 1988.

Engel HM. *How to Delegate.* Houston: Gulf Publishing, 1983.

Erikson K. *Encounters.* New Haven: Yale University Press, 1989.

Evens R, Jost RG, Evens R Jr. Economic and utilization analysis of magnetic resonance imaging units in the United States in 1985. *American Journal of Roentgenology* 145:393-398, 1985.

Field MJ, Lohr KN (eds). *Clinical Practice Guidelines: Directions for a New Program.* Washington, DC: National Academy Press, 1990.

Fleischer AC, James AE Jr. *Real-Time Sonography.* Norwalk, CT: Appleton-Century-Crofts, 1984.

Fleischer AC, James AE Jr (eds). *Diagnostic Sonography: Principles and Clinical Applications.* Philadelphia: WB Saunders, 1989.

Fleischer AC, Romero R, Manning FA, Jeanty P, James AE Jr (eds). *The Principles and Practice of Ultrasonography in Obstetrics and Gynecology,* 4th edition. Norwalk, CT: Appleton & Lange, 1991.

Freudenberg HJ. *Burn Out.* New York, Bantam Books, 1989.

Friedman M, Rosenman R. *Type A Behavior and Your Heart.* Greenwich, CT: Fawcett, 1974.

Fulgham RL. *All I Really Need to Know I Learned in Kindergarten: Uncommon Thoughts on Common Things.* New York: Ivy Books, 1986.

Geneen H. *Managing.* New York: Avon Books, 1984.

Ginzburg E. The monetarization of medical care. *New England Journal of Medicine* 310:1162-1165, 1984.

Goodman C, Baratz SR (eds). *Improving Consensus Development for Health Care Technology Assessment: An International Perspective.* Washington, DC: National Academy Press, 1990.

Gordon O. White, M.D. v. Rockingham Radiologists, Ltd., 820 F2d 98 (4th Cir. 1987).

Greer A. The state of the art versus the state of the science. *International Journal of Technology Assessment in Health Care* 4:5-26, 1988.

Hanson PG. *Stress for Success.* New York: Ballantine, 1992.

Harris TA. *I'm Okay--You're Okay.* New York: Harper and Row, 1969.

Harvey IM, Roberts CJ. Clinical guidelines, medical litigation, and the current medical defense system. *Lancet* 1:145-147, 1987.

Havighurst CC. Practice guidelines as legal standards governing physician liability. *Law and Contemporary Problems* 54(2):87-117, 1991.

Hawking S. *A Brief History of Time*. New York: Bantam Books, 1988.

Heider J. *Tao of Leadership*. New York: Bantam Books, 1985.

Heller R. *The Super Chiefs*. New York: Penguin Books, 1992.

Hersey P, Blanchard KH. *Management of Organizational Behavior*, 6th edition. Englewood, NJ: Prentice-Hall, 1993.

Hillman AL. Health maintenance organizations, financial incentives, and physicians' judgments. *Annals of Internal Medicine* 112:891-893, 1990.

Hillman AL, Pauly MV, Kerstein JJ. How do financial incentives affect physicians' clinical decisions and the financial performance of health maintenance organizations? *New England Journal of Medicine* 321:86-92, 1989.

Hillman BJ, Fajardo LL, Witzke DB, Cardenas D, Irion M, Fluginiti JV. Influences affecting radiologists' choices of academic or private practice careers. *Radiology* 174:561-564, 1990.

Hirshfeld EB. Practice parameters and the malpractice liability of physicians. *Journal of the American Medical Association* 263:1556-1562, 1990.

Hunt DV. *Managing for Quality*. Homewood, IL: Business One Irwin, 1993.

Hyde v. Jefferson Parish Hospital District No. 2, 686 F2d 286 (5th Cir. 1982), cert granted, 51 USLW 3649 (1983).

Jacoby I. The consensus development program of the National Institutes of Health: current practices and historical perspectives. *International Journal of Technology Assessment in Health Care* 1:420-432, 1985.

Jacoby I. Evidence and consensus. *Journal of the American Medical Association* 259:3039, 1988.

Jacoby I, Rose M. Transfer of information and its impact on medical practice: the U.S. experience. *International Journal of Technology Assessment in Health Care* 2:107-115, 1986.

James AE Jr. The chairman of radiology: a changing profile. *Administrative Radiology* 6(11):33-47, 1987.

James AE Jr (ed). *Legal Medicine with Special Reference to Diagnostic Imaging*. Baltimore: Urban & Schwarzenberg, 1980.

James AE Jr (ed). *Medical/Legal Issues for Radiologists*. Chicago: Precept Press, 1987.

James AE Jr. A physician's opportunity to contribute in the arts. *The Pharos of Alpha Omega Alpha* 48(3):18-21, 1985.

James AE Jr. Using art to humanize the medical experience. *Administrative Radiology* 7(1):52-54, 1988.

James AE Jr, Anderson JH, Higgins CB (eds). *Digital Image Processing in Radiology*. Baltimore: Williams & Wilkins, 1984.

James AE Jr, Baum S. Procurement of technology: an ethical dilemma. *Investigative Radiology* 22:148, 1987.

James AE Jr, Chapman JE, Carroll F, Pendergrass HP, Fleischer AC, Zaner R, Sloan F, Greeson T. Ethical choices in high technology medicine: current dilemmas in diagnostic imaging. *Health Care Instrumentation* 1:158-167, 1986.

James AE Jr, Curran WJ, Pendergrass HP, Chapman JE. Academic radiology, turf conflict and antitrust laws. *Investigative Radiology* 25:200-202, 1990.

James AE Jr, Erickson JJ, Carroll FE, Pickens DR, Zaner R, Chapman J. Medical imaging management: practical, legal and ethical considerations. *Computers in Biology and Medicine* 16(4):247-257, 1986.

James AE Jr, Greeson T, Price RR, Pendergrass HP, Carroll FE, Partain CL Zaner R, Hamilton RJ, Chapman J. Legal and ethical issues in a technologic discipline: new times, new choices. *Investigative Radiology* 21:673-677, 1986.

James AE Jr, Mazer MJ, Dawson RC III. Medical legal issues in interventional radiology. In: Kadir S (ed): *Current Practice of Interventional Radiology*. Philadelphia: BC Decker Inc., 7-11, 1991.

James AE Jr, Partain CL Heller RM, Patton JA, Price RR. Can we administrate academics? Preserving the biomedical research enterprise in medical imaging. *Investigative Radiology* 24:815-816, 1989.

James AE Jr, Pendergrass HP, Robinson R, Hamilton RJ, Rollo FD, Hollowell E. Exclusive physician contracts in hospitals: precedent cases for radiologic practice. *Administrative Radiology* 6(5):28-31, 1987.

James AE, Perry S, Warner SE, Chapman JE, Zaner RM. The diffusion of medical technology: free enterprise and regulatory models in the USA. *Journal of Medical Ethics* 17:150-155, 1991.

James AE Jr, Perry S, Zaner RM, Chapman JE. Are medical imaging centers a cause for societal concern? *Humane Medicine* 4:1, 1988.

James AE Jr, Price RR, Sloan F, Zaner R, Chapman J. Certain social considerations in abandoning high technology medical imaging. *Health Matrix* 5(3):31-34, 1987.

James AE Jr, Price RR, Stephens WH, Patton JA, Partain CL. Continuing the momentum: biotechnological research in the 1990s. *Applied Radiology* 18(10):27-28, 1989.

James AE Jr, Sloan F, Blumstein J, Winfield AC, Pendergrass HP. Certificate-of-need in an antitrust context. *Journal of Health Politics, Policy and Law* 8:314-319, 1983.

James AE Jr, Sloan FA, Hamilton R, Chick B, Zaner RM, Pendergrass HP, Stephens WH, Quimby CW Jr, Greeson T. Antitrust aspects of exclusive contracts in medical imaging. *Radiology* 156:237-241, 1985.

James AE, Squire LF. *Nuclear Radiology*. Philadelphia: WB Saunders, 1973.

James AE Jr, Zaner RM, Chapman JE, Partain CL Technology and "turf": medicine in conflict. *Humane Medicine* 6:264-268, 1990.

Kirsch MM. *How to Get Off the Fast Track*. New York: Harper Books, 1991.

Konik v. Champlain Valley Physicians Hospital, 733 F2d 1007 (2nd Cir. 1984).

Korda M. *Power*. New York: Random House, 1975.

Kushner H. *When Bad Things Happen to Good People*. New York: Random House, 1987.
Lakein A. *How to Control Your Time and Your Life*. New York: Penguin Books, 1973.
Landrum GN. *Profiles of Genius*. Buffalo: Prometheus Books, 1993.
Leavitt HJ, Bahrami H. *Managerial Psychology*. Chicago: University of Chicago Press, 1988.
Levinson DJ. *The Seasons of a Man's Life*. New York: Knopf, 1978.
Lewisburg Community Hospital, Inc. v. David Alfredson, M.D., 805 Southwest 2nd 756 (1991).
Liddy G. *Will*. New York: St. Martin's Press, 1980.
Locke E. *The Essence of Leadership*. New York: MacMillan, 1991.
Lohr KN, Yordy KD, Thier SO. Current issues in quality of care. *Health Affairs* 7:5-18, 1988.
Lomas J. The consensus process and evidence dissemination. *Canadian Medical Association Journal* 134:1340-1341, 1986.
Lomas J, Anderson GM, Domnick-Pierre K, Vayda E, Enkin MW, Hannah WJ. Do practice guidelines guide practice? The effect of a consensus statement on the practice of physicians. *New England Journal of Medicine* 321:1306-1311, 1989.
Lowry KM. How Japan vaccinates its CEOs. *Business Week*, April 22, 1991.
Lynch P. *Beating the Street*. New York: Simon & Schuster, 1993.
Mackay H. *Swim with the Sharks without Being Eaten Alive*. New York: Ivy Books, 1988.
Mallinger AE, DeWyze J. *Too Perfect: Control*. New York: Ballantine, 1992.
Mann NR. *The Keys to Excellence*, 3rd edition. Los Angeles: Prestwick, 1992.
Manuel BM. Professional liability: a no-fault solution. *New England Journal of Medicine* 322:627-631, 1990.
Matloff M (editor). *The Civil War: A Concise Military History of the War Between the States*, 1861-1865. New York: Promontory Press, 1978.
McCormack M. *What They Don't Teach You at Harvard Business School*. New York: Bantam Books, 1984.
McCormack M. *What They Still Don't Teach at Harvard Business School*. New York: Bantam Books, 1989.
McDonald G. *Ordering Your Private World*. Nashville: Thomas Nelson, 1975.
McNeil BJ, Pauker SG. Decision analysis for public health: principles and illustrations. *Annual Review of Public Health* 5:135-161, 1984.
Meyer C. *Fast Cycle Time*. New York: MacMillan, 1993.
Miller WC. *The Creative Edge*. Reading, MA: Addison-Wesley, 1986.
Morton MS. *The Corporation of the 1990's*. New York: Oxford Press, 1991.
Moyers W. *Healing and the Mind*. New York: Doubleday, 1993.
Mullan F, Jacoby I. The town meeting for technology: the maturation of consensus conferences. *Journal of the American Medical Association* 254:1068-1072, 1985.
Naisbitt J, Aburdene P. *Megatrends 2000*. New York: Avon Books, 1990.

Naisbitt J, Aburdene P. *Reinventing the Corporation*. Boston: Warner Books, 1985.

National Academy of Sciences. *Responsible Science*. Washington, DC: National Academy Press, 1992.

Nelson CA, Cavey RD. *Ethics Leadership*. Croton-on-Hudson, NY: North Ruci Press, 1991.

Nouwen HJ. *Reaching Out*. New York: Doubleday, 1975.

Partain CL, Price RR, Patton JA, Kulkarni MV, James AE Jr (eds). *Magnetic Resonance Imaging*, 2nd ed. Philadelphia: WB Saunders, 1988.

Pascale RT, Athos AG. *The Art of Japanese Management*. New York: Simon & Schuster, 1981.

Peck MS. *The Road Less Travelled*. New York: Simon & Schuster, 1989.

Peck MS. *People of the Lie*. New York: Simon & Schuster, 1992.

Pellegrino ED. Rationing health care: the ethics of medical gatekeeping. *Journal of Contemporary Law Policy* 2:23-45, 1986.

Pennington R, Bockman M. *On My Honor I Will*. New York: Warner Books, 1992.

Perry S. Consensus development: an historical note. *International Journal of Technology Assessment in Health Care* 4:481-484, 1988.

Perry S. The NIH consensus development a decade later. *New England Journal of Medicine* 317:485-488, 1987.

Peter LJ, Hull R. *The Peter Principle*. New York: Bantam Books, 1970.

Peters T. *Thriving on Chaos*. New York: Alfred A. Knopf, 1987.

Peters T, Austin H. *A Passion for Excellence*. New York: Random House, 1985.

Peters T, Townsend R. *Excellence in the Organization*. Chicago: Nightingale, 1990.

Peters TJ, Waterman RH Jr. *In Search of Excellence: Lessons from America's Best-Run Companies*. New York: Warner Books, 1982.

Phillips DT. *Lincoln on Leadership*. New York: Warner Books, 1992.

Price RR, Rollo FD, Monahan WG, James AE Jr. *Digital Radiography: A Focus on Clinical Utility*. New York: Grune & Stratton, 1982.

Relman AS. Dealing with conflicts of interest. *New England Journal of Medicine* 313:749-751, 1985.

Relman AS. Changing the malpractice liability system. *New England Journal of Medicine* 322:626-627, 1990.

Reynolds RA, Rizzo JA, Gonzalez ML The cost of medical professional liability. *Journal of the American Medical Association* 257:2776-2781, 1987.

Ringa V, Blondel B, Breart G. Ultrasound in obstetrics: do the published evaluative studies justify its routine use? *International Journal of Epidemiology* 18:489-497, 1989.

Rlazinga NS, Caspari AF, van Everdingen JJE. Contribution of medical decision-making to consensus development conferences. *Health Policy* 8:339-346, 1987.

Roberts W. *Victory Secrets of Attila the Hun*. New York: Bantam Books, 1992.

Robertson T, Gatignon H. The diffusion of high technology innovations: a marketing perspective. In: Pennings J, Buitendam A (eds). *New Technology as Organizational Innovation: The Development and Diffusion of Microelectronics.* New York: Ballinger, 1987.

Rogers RM, Larsen JK, Lowe CU. The consensus development process of medical technologies: a cross-cultural comparison of Sweden and the United States. *Journal of the American Medical Association* 248:1880-1882, 1982.

Roper W, Winkenwerder W, Hackbarth G, Krakauer H. Effectiveness in health care: an initiative to evaluate and improve medical practice. *New England Journal of Medicine* 319:1197-1202, 1989.

Sandler MP, Patton JA, Shaff MI, Powers TA, Partain CL *Correlative Imaging: Nuclear Medicine, Magnetic Resonance, Computed Tomography, Ultrasound.* Baltimore: Williams & Wilkins, 1989.

Sayles LR. *The Working Leader.* New York: MacMillan, 1993.

Schuller R. *Success Is Never Ending, Failure Never Final.* New York: Bantam Books, 1990.

Scott M, Rothman H. *Companies with a Conscience.* New York: Carol Publishing Company, 1992.

Seidman WL Skancke SL. *Productivity.* New York: Simon & Schuster, 1989.

Seligman MEP. *Learned Optimism.* New York: Simon & Schuster, 1991.

Senge PM. *The Fifth Discipline.* New York, Doubleday, 1992.

Shapero A. *Managing Professional People.* New York: MacMillan, 1985.

Sheehy G. *Passages: Predictable Crises of Adult Life.* New York: Dutton, 1976.

Showstack JA, Schroeder SA, Matsumoto MF. Changes in the use of medical technologies, 1971-1977: a study of 10 inpatient diagnoses. *New England Journal of Medicine* 306:706-712, 1982.

Solomon R. *Ethics and Excellence.* New York: Oxford Press, 1992.

Sonnenfeld J. *The Hero's Farewell.* New York: Oxford Press, 1988.

Strauss HW, Pitt B, James AE. *Cardiovascular Nuclear Medicine.* St. Louis: CV Mosby, 1974.

Suters ET. *The Unnatural Act of Management.* New York: Harper Collins, 1992.

Thorpe KE, Hendricks A, Garnick D, Donelan K, Newhouse JP. Reducing the number of uninsured by subsidizing employment based health insurance: results from a pilot study. *Journal of the American Medical Association* 267:945-953, 1992.

Thurow L *The Zero Sum Society.* Boston: Warner Books, 1992.

Tichy NM. *Managing Strategic Change.* New York: John Wiley and Sons, 1993.

Tournier P. *The Healing of Persons.* New York: Harper and Row, 1983.

Tournier P. *The Strong and the Weak.* Louisville, KY: Westminster, 1976.

Townsend R. *Further Up the Organization.* New York: Harper & Row, 1984.

Tucker RB. *Managing the Future.* New York: Berkley Publishing Company, 1991.

Viorst J. *Necessary Losses.* New York: Fawcett, 1987.

Walton M. *The Deming Management Method.* New York: Putnam, 1986.

Ward GC, Burns R, Burns K. *The Civil War.* New York: Alfred C. Knopf, 1990.

Weiler P, Brennan TA. Medical malpractice. In: *A Call for Action.* Washington, DC: The Pepper Commission on Comprehensive Health Care, 1990: vol 2.

Wennberg JE. Outcomes research, cost containment, and the fear of health care rationing. *New England Journal of Medicine* 323:1202-1204, 1990.

Wortman PM, Vinokur A, Sechrest L. Do consensus conferences work? A process evaluation of the NIH consensus development program. *Journal of Health Politics, Policy and Law* 13:469-498, 1988.

INDEX